AGELESS ATHLETE SERIES

RUNNING
Past 50

Richard Benyo

Human Kinetics

Library of Congress Cataloging-In-Publication Data

Benyo, Richard
    Running past 50/ by Richard Benyo.
        p.   cm.   — (Ageless athlete series)
    Includes index.
    ISBN 0-88011-705-2
    1. Running for the aged.   I. Title.   II. Series.
    GV1061.18.A35B46   1998   97-52054
    613.7'172'0846—dc21   CIP

ISBN: 0-88011-705-2

Developmental Editor: Syd Slobodnik; **Assistant Editors:** Katy Patterson, Cynthia McEntire, and Erin Cler; **Copyeditor:** Jim Burns; **Graphic Designer:** Robert Reuther; **Graphic Artist:** Joe Bellis; **Photo Manager:** Boyd LaFoon; **Cover Designer:** Keith Blomberg; **Printer:** United Graphics

Human Kinetics books are available at special discounts for bulk purchase. Special editions or book excerpts can also be created to specification. For details, contact the Special Sales Manager at Human Kinetics.

Printed in the United States of America   10 9 8 7 6 5 4 3 2 1

Human Kinetics
Web site: http://www.humankinetics.com/

United States: Human Kinetics, P.O. Box 5076, Champaign, IL 61825-5076
1-800-747-4457
e-mail: humank@hkusa.com

Canada: Human Kinetics, Box 24040, Windsor, ON N8Y 4Y9
1-800-465-7301 (in Canada only)
e-mail: humank@hkcanada.com

Europe: Human Kinetics, P.O. Box IW14, Leeds LS16 6TR, United Kingdom
(44) 1132 781708
e-mail: humank@hkeurope.com

Australia: Human Kinetics, 57A Price Avenue, Lower Mitcham, South Australia 5062
(088) 277 1555
e-mail: humank@hkaustralia.com

New Zealand: Human Kinetics, P.O. Box 105-231, Auckland 1
(09) 523 3462
e-mail: humank@hknewz.com

This book is for Walt "The Ancient Marathoner" Stack and Dick "The Locomotive" Collins, two guys who, like fine wine, just got better the more they aged and ran.

Contents

Preface

Familiarity breeds contempt. Anyone who's ever teetered on the edge of a rut, or who's slid down its slippery slopes, knows just how accurate those three words are. Anything we do on a regular basis, whether loving a mate or stamp collecting or photographing sunsets, needs constant attention and renewal if it is to remain fresh and, by remaining fresh, maintain our devotion.

The same is true of a running program, especially as the realities of aging—no matter how glacial—present us with the only too obvious fact that for most intents and purposes, our days of setting Personal Records are behind us—unless we pursue them into the age-group structure.

Nowhere along the calendar pages of life does this reality come with a bigger, juicier red X than at our 50th birthday. Most of us who are even marginally active on the physical front have managed to obliterate, at least in our own minds and bodies, the traditional assumption that 40 years of age marks the onset of "middle age." These days, as we push back all sorts of boundaries, 50 more realistically marks middle age. After all, barring some catastrophic occurrence, we're biologically constructed to make it safely into triple digits.

There is growing evidence that Jack LaLanne's half-century-old adage, "Use it or lose it," is firmly grounded in science. The most dramatic proof from the past decade that the aging body is prepared to be as frail or as tough as we demand it to be came from Maria A. Fiatarone's study at the U.S. Department of Agriculture Human Nutrition Research Center on Aging at Tufts University in Boston. "Ten frail, institutionalized men and women, averaging 90 years of age, took part in an eight-week program of high-intensity resistance training of the leg muscles," Dr. Peter Wood of Stanford reported in his 1992 annual summary in the *Encyclopedia Britannica Medical and*

Health Annual. "Strength increased by 174%; muscle area, measured by a computed tomography (CT) scan, increased by 9%; and mobility substantially improved. Two participants who had previously relied on canes for walking were able to dispense with them after the training program."

For those who've been regularly using the huge muscle bunches of the legs in an ongoing running program through the 50s, 60s, 70s, and beyond, that startling news is no news. We realize by monitoring our workouts on familiar courses that aging does exact a bit of a toll, but it is in spare change, not large coin.

The great danger to our running as we age is not the fact that our performances erode in very minor ways, but that we become complacent about our running programs to the point that they take on the dull sheen of monotony, while we simultaneously pay little attention to adjustments we can and should make to our programs to keep them vital and refreshing, in the process protecting ourselves from injuries. Left to itself, shrunk in importance by the realization that aging is attempting to erode us away, a running program can easily become pedestrian and lackluster, a mere prophylactic in our day instead of a shining pinnacle.

To avoid this, we must realize that a regular running program consistently infused with creativity on top of a foundation of common sense can serve as the restorative spring from which we draw sustenance to keep us young on a cellular level and vital in all areas, including psychologically and spiritually. Physical inactivity, quite simply, extinguishes an individual's spirit.

Must we make adjustments to our running programs as we age? Certainly. But those adjustments come in the form of minor compromises, not major capitulations. The beauty of running is that a sport so simple (mission: place one foot in front of the other, then alternate) is so versatile. We have the power to customize our running to our changing lifestyle, or we can soup up our running program to the point where it drives and nourishes that lifestyle.

This book is not written for a 50+-year-old who is finally taking up running. There are dozens of excellent books available for the beginning runner. Instead, this book is directed at those 50+ runners who have been plugging away steadily at this simplest yet most complex of all sports for a decade or two or three. It is for those runners who find this juncture in life a good point from which to evaluate and perhaps recharge their running program in the wake of the hard realization that our fastest races may well be behind us, but that we still have plenty of quality miles left to us.

In this book we'll take a long run together during which we'll review the physical changes that have caught up to us. We'll determine which we are obliged by nature to accept and which we can roll right over, and we'll adjust our running programs accordingly.

We'll review the growing mass of scientific data gleaned over the decades from research centered specifically on 50+ athletes by The Fifty-Plus Fitness Association, formerly The Fifty-Plus Runners' Association (Fifty-Plus Fitness, P.O. Box D, Stanford, CA 94309; 415-323-6160).

We'll meet ordinary and extraordinary 50+ runners who by determination or talent or both have reset the bar for all of us.

We'll consider simple but effective methods of infusing our running programs with new life by making adjustments that range from profoundly simple to ambitiously complex. We'll review the four basic training elements and see how we can proportion them best to make our running safer and more satisfying.

We'll reexamine our long-term running goals and see where we can infuse them with new meaning while enjoying the process to the maximum.

But most importantly we'll check out the potential our running program, like the legendary Fountain of Youth, holds to play a physically and psychologically rejuvenating role throughout the second half of our aerobic century.

Acknowledgments

A book that reflects on several decades of running and anticipates a few more decades evolves more than gets created. This book's evolution was helped along by thousands of miles of running with thousands of runners in hundreds of locations, but in retrospect, some running companions stand out as having had a very real bearing on its directions: Bill Howard and Larry Tunis, Bob Anderson, Joe Henderson, Joe Oakes, Rhonda Provost, Tom and Nancy Crawford, Jean Ennis, Ruth Anderson, Norm and Helen Klein. Special acknowledgment, also, to Brian Holding, whose valiant efforts on behalf of *The Exercise Fix* led to so many subsequent opportunities.

PART

I

The Machine

1

Evaluating

"There are those who believe that a regimen of long-distance running, swimming, or cycling will solve all ills and wipe out any possibility of heart disease. They have become victims of a syndrome that raises exercise to an undeserved level of superpanacea."

—Dr. Kenneth H. Cooper
Running Without Fear, 1985

Mortality is a pretty scary thing. Fortunately for our psychological well-being, consciousness of mortality is usually reserved for the second half of life, when we are theoretically more able to deal with it. When we were young, immortality was our philosophy. We were invincible and we approached life accordingly.

At some point in that stretch of life known as "middle age," an appreciation of mortality snuck up on us. We went to a barbecue at a friend's house, played some volleyball, drank a little too much wine, and could barely get out of bed the next day. We ruefully reflected that in our early 20s we could party three nights in a row, stay up until 3 A.M. to finish a term paper, and awake after two hours sleep refreshed and ready to take on the world.

This new arrangement sounds like a loser's game, but there is a very major upside. From midlife on, we learn to appreciate life more, just as life seems to begin to unreel at a frightening pace. Of course, the best way to maximize the many decades of life left to us is to make certain we are fit and healthy enough to enjoy it physically, mentally, and spiritually. Which is where our running comes in: it is the physically simple yet physiologically complex tool we use to allow us to extract the most from ourselves and our world.

Considering that the human body was designed with the largest bones and muscles in the legs, it requires no great intellectual leap to assume that the legs were designed to transport us through and around our world. After all, if we were designed to sit around doing nothing all day, our rumps would be designed so they'd become more supple and well-toned the more we sat.

Running, a basic and natural activity that enjoys a well-documented history as the primary human mode of transportation, is profoundly simple yet offers a virtual barrage of benefits to its devotees: strong heart and lungs, strong legs, low blood pressure, lower-than-average body fat, low resting heart rate, increased energy reserves, increased bone density, higher brain function due to regular exercise-induced oxygenation of the brain, regular doses of psychological equanimity, greater physical confidence and self-esteem, less overall physical degeneration, and so on.

It is not, however, a cure-all, a magic bullet. Runners still die of heart attacks, though much less often than the rest of the population. (A February 1997 report in the *New England Journal of Medicine* indicates that runners who log 40 miles per week decrease their chance of heart disease by 30 percent.) Runners incur cancer and die from it like any other mortal human beings, although there is some indication that regular aerobic exercise helps delay or prevent certain cancers.

Runners occasionally suffer mental meltdowns just like regular walking-around or sitting-around people but typically not as often, due in part to the fact that they've got far too much to do to have time for a breakdown and also because regular aerobic exercise has been shown to bestow a variety of psychological benefits.

So much so, in fact, that in 1984 Michael L. Sachs and Gary W. Buffone published a collection of "running therapy" studies under the title *Running as Therapy: An Integrated Approach* (University of Nebraska Press, Lincoln & London). The book was republished in 1997 as part of The Jason Aronson Publishers' Master Works Series.

As early as 1978 (Frederich Harper, *Journal of Physical Education*), experiments with groups of college students placed on a five-days-a-week running program showed overwhelmingly positive effects: "Post-test measures indicated a significant decrease in state anxiety, a moderate decrease in trait anxiety, and a moderate improvement in self-concept. Moreover, self-reports from the students themselves indicated improved ability to sleep and relax, increased physical and mental energy, improved sexual appreciation, ability to cope with stress, mental alertness, and self-confidence, increased capacity for work, and greater appreciation of health." When we run, we do not become immortal—it only occasionally feels like we do.

Let's Get Physical

Considering how much hard work runners put into whipping themselves into good physical condition, you'd figure they'd be elbowing each other out of the way to be the first in line each year to take a physical examination in order to verify and document just how healthy they are, to pick up early warnings of potential physical problems that they can then head off, and just to show off against the unfit masses of people in their age group.

But when it comes to physical examinations, most runners can be lumped with the rest of the population: they drag their feet and only go for an exam when physically dragged there. The reluctance to be pricked and probed, weighed and measured on an annual basis comes from one of two stances:

1. One of arrogance: "I'm a runner, and therefore immune to all that afflicts mere mortals."
2. One of fear: "What I don't know won't hurt me."

The latter may be the rationalization Jim Fixx employed when he refused Dr. Ken Cooper's offer to do a complete physical including a stress test on him while he was visiting Dr. Cooper in Dallas while researching a book project six months before his death.

This philosophy is surprisingly widespread. I grew up in eastern Pennsylvania, in the wake of King Coal's reign. Many of the residents of my town were only one generation removed from European immigrants who came to America to work the mines. There was a philosophy that was extremely widespread and that I never understood: if a person was taken to a doctor for an examination and he or she had a life-threatening disease (emphysema caused by breathing tons of coal dust was a common medical condition among males), in the wake of the examination, the physician would consult with the immediate family, but not with the patient. If there *was* a life-threatening problem, which emphysema certainly is, the family's stance was to not let the patient know he was dying. Which I always found unfair to the patient. What if the poor sot wanted to get his life in order before he died? Besides, I think most people who are dying already suspect as much. Certainly, it was mass denial of the inevitable, an inability to deal with a family member's mortality, but it was also a stance of "What he doesn't know won't hurt him."

The tendency of many usually correct-thinking people to refuse an annual physical examination is outrageous when you consider the extent to which the typical American male will go to have the family automobile evaluated and rejuvenated before leaving on the annual vacation. We take better care of our cars and our pets than we do of ourselves.

Many experts theorize that the reason men die earlier in life than women is not because the tendency is biologically inherent, but because in general men avoid the doctor's office like the plague while women tend to visit the doctor with more frequency.

Beyond menopause, women catch up to men in the incidence of heart disease, and with heart disease the prime killer of adult Americans, its gradual incursion into our lives should be monitored carefully.

Practical advice can't be stated any simpler than this: men and women over 50 should have an annual physical examination.

Early Detection

Additionally, since prostate cancer in men and breast cancer in women increase significantly beyond middle age, the annual physical exam allows your doctor to detect any potential problems in those areas. Early detection remains the best line of defense against both of these types of cancer.

Physical exams these days are quick, easy, and the blood and urine tests yield an increasingly fascinating array of information. For those who've managed to regularly avoid a physical, here's what you're missing:

The physical exam itself takes roughly 10 minutes. You're weighed, blood pressure is taken, the doctor listens to your heart and lungs, pokes and probes here and there to check things like your liver, asks a half-dozen questions. The doctor checks female clients for lumps in the breasts, something women should be checking for themselves every few weeks. Male clients are checked for abnormal size of the prostate, something they can't readily do for themselves.

You are then sent to the lab where you leave a urine sample and blood is drawn. Within a week or so the lab sends the results to your doctor, who examines them, calls you with those results, and then sends a copy. I like to think of the arrival of the lab results in the same way as I regard the arrival of a finisher's certificate from a road race. How'd I do? Especially, how'd I do against other people in my age group?

The lab results are relatively easy for the average person to understand. The report lists all the tests, your specific result, and then gives a normal range. If there are any abnormalities in your results, you'll be able to easily pick them out because they are flagged by the lab.

For a long-distance runner, it is not unusual for the lab report to indicate that there is a trace of blood in the urine. There have been numerous theories expounded over the years attempting to explain this phenomenon, the most often cited simply being that the repetitive jarring that occurs during the process of running slightly bruises the bladder walls if the bladder is empty. The solution seems to be to drink a big glass of water before you go running—which is good advice whether you've got blood in your urine or not.

Blood Work

The blood tests provide some very important numbers. Everyone should know where they stand relative to cholesterol, a reliable indicator of plaque buildup in the arteries. The proportion of high-density lipoproteins to low-density lipoproteins is as important as the raw cholesterol number. High-density lipoprotein is the "good" cholesterol; it acts to scrub low-density lipoprotein (the "bad" cholesterol) off the artery walls. Physical activities such as distance running elevate the level of high-density lipoproteins.

The blood test also indicates whether or not you are leaning toward anemia, which could have a profound (read that negative) effect upon your running performance. And, for males, the prostate PSA test that is now routinely done on blood lab workups is a very effective early-warning system of potential prostate problems.

Back on the urine test, one test that I can't help but smile at every time I encounter it is "bilirubin." The first time I heard the term I thought it was a kid I vaguely recall who used to sit behind me in the third grade. Bilirubin is actually one of the major end-products of hemoglobin decomposition, which is a process that is ongoing. Red blood cells have a life span of roughly 120 days. When they finally break down, bilirubin is released in various combinations. Some 5 percent is passed from the kidneys to the urine. Measuring bilirubin indicates kidney function as well as warns of problems such as jaundice if the count is unusually high.

If you have any questions whatsoever about your test results, call your physician for an explanation. If your doctor did find something unusual, it would have been pointed out—along with a solution—during the follow-up call.

The best way to remember to have your physical each year is to tie it in to some significant event, such as your birthday. And keep your lab test results safely tucked away for comparison's sake as you retake the test each year. If you keep your race results in a file, or if you keep a running journal, tuck your lab test results there, so they are easily accessible.

Your good lab results have enormous potential in other areas. When you go to a boring cocktail party where people are running through a litany of their current maladies, you can bring the conversation to a crashing halt by cheerfully piping up with how you just received the results of your annual physical, you're fit as a fiddle, never felt better, how 'bout them HDLs? No sense letting the good results of all those hard miles go unrecognized.

Bad Bod, Bad Brain

Since these are terms that will be cropping up at a furious rate throughout this book, this would be a logical juncture to mention that for the 50+ runner, there are two major areas of concern, either or both of which can jeopardize or undermine an ongoing running program, and both of which can be brought under control. They go by various descriptive terms, but I tend to simplify them as Bad Bod Syndrome and Bad Brain Disease.

Bad Bod Syndrome

Bad Bod Syndrome refers to the simple fact that as we age, body systems weaken or become increasingly inefficient. This is a process that is inevitable. But it is also a process that can be retarded by a regular physical exercise program. It can, in fact, be *greatly* retarded by regular aerobic exercise. But even with the most perfect exercise program ever conceived, the process still continues, if only glacially.

Where runners run into trouble is when their body turns 50 years old while their mind remains stuck at 19. Consequently, there is a tendency to push the maturing body as though it is forever young. The deterioration of the function of various body systems becomes noticeable at age 40, yet many runners continue to push their bodies without respect for the processes that nature is forcing upon them. They whip their body through workouts as though it were still 30 years old. The consequences are inevitable: the body breaks down, usually in the form of overuse injuries. Which frustrates the runner, so he or she continues to work out in spite of the injury, or else grants it time to heal, only to jump right back into a workout routine appropriate to a 30-year-old but destructive to a 50-year-old.

In its way, this whipping the body is a form of arrogance, as in, "I'll show this damned body who's in charge!" Ultimately, we don't show our maturing body anything except how to become expert at becoming injured.

As we age we must respect the fact that our body is changing, that it is slowing, that it requires more time to recuperate than it did 10 or 15 years ago. The encouraging fact that we need to recognize and respect is that the aging but exercising body *does not rapidly lose its ability to perform incredible feats*. What it does lose is its ability to readily bounce back from hard workouts or races.

It is still possible to run the 50- or 60- or 70-year-old body through track workouts that it ran 20 or 30 years before; the times will not be quite as fast, but the times will still be surprisingly impressive. What the body requires in return for its ability to astound is additional recuperation time before it is again subjected to a hard workout.

Too often we deny our body the respect it deserves and, if we continue to make outrageous, unreasonable demands upon it, it in turn has no choice but to rebel, presenting us with a sure sign of its mortality—an injury. It is simply a fact of life: the older we are, the more prone we are to injury. There is no way around this. Body systems become compromised and become more prone to breakdowns. This is a fact intelligent veteran runners recognize early on and which they accommodate. Make provisions for the additional recuperation your body requests before it begins exacting its toll.

Run five days a week instead of six or seven. Take three or four weeks off during a naturally-occurring "down" time of the year in order to allow minor, microscopic tears and rips in the muscles time to heal before again running them through demanding workouts. Your body will thank—and reward—you.

Mind Over Matters

The other major area of concern which we will address in nearly every chapter of this book is Bad Brain Disease. Bad Brain Disease, simply put, is lack of mental motivation, which can ultimately lead to burnout.

If you've been running long distances for the past 20 years, that's a lot of miles on those legs, and a lot of going to the mental and spiritual well to whip up the motivation to get out the door to do workouts that at times you perhaps weren't so keen on. The workout you looked forward to 12 years ago may today draw a weary sigh from you that translates: "Aaah, geez, not that one again. . . ."

The body goes where the brain directs it. It is human nature that after directing the body to go out the door for a workout 4,500 times over the past 15 years (300 days x 15 years), the process is getting a little old. Especially if Bad Brain hooks up with Bad Bod and Bad Bod says, "Man, I'm run down. Gimme a break, huh?"

HELEN KLEIN

In 1988, *Runner's World* magazine declared Helen Klein to be the "Woman of the Century," (i.e., 100-milers). To many both outside and inside running, Helen Klein, a retired nurse in her mid-60s, seemed an unlikely choice for "Woman of the Century." She didn't even take up running until she was 55 years old, for goodness' sake.

Helen Klein, 75 years old on November 27, 1997, makes the point best herself in the inspirational speeches she is increasingly giving to groups around the country: "I'm nothing extraordinary. I was—and am—just like you are. We all have tremendous poten-tial, but potential is an inac-tive state. Potential must be turned to realization. And we realize our potential by tap-ping it. But tapping it can transform our lives. I've seen it happen numerous times. It doesn't have to be running we're talking about, but there are some of you out there who have the potential to be tremendous runners. You just haven't activated your running potential yet."

Helen Klein activated her potential in 1978 when she began running with abso-lutely no previous experi-ence in the sport. In fact, she had no previous experience in any sports. But pretty soon she was challenging herself to enter 10K races and then 10-mile races. In her first 10-mile race, she placed dead last. But she persisted. Even-tually she found that relative to other women—and men— her age, she was very com-petitive.

Caught up in the wave of racing, Helen entered ever longer races, where the older runner has an advantage of knowing a thing or two about pacing. With no athletic experience, she also decided to try the triathlon, but not just any triathlon. She began to train for the famed Hawaii Ironman Triathlon, taking masters swim lessons and learning how to race a bicycle. She entered and completed the Ironman, one of the oldest competitors to ever take on the challenge.

But it was in running—very long-distance running—where Helen's focus and talent began to shine. The mother of four, grandmother of nine, and great-grandmother of three currently holds more than 75 world and American records in her age group and in single-age categories for the following distances: 50K, 50 miles, 100K, 100 miles, 24 hours, 48 hours, five-day, and six-day runs.

She's completed 105 ultramarathons and 50 marathons. In the spring of 1995, she completed the grueling Marathon Des Sables, a 145-mile stage race across the Sahara Desert in Morocco where competitors carry their own supplies; two weeks later she competed in and completed the first annual Eco Challenge in Utah, a 370-mile multi-sport race where her four teammates were each nearly one-third her age. Her accomplishments won her the coveted ESPN Arete Award for courage in sports.

One of her most spectacular feats came in 1989 when, at age 66, she became one of the first women to complete what is known as the Grand Slam of Ultrarunning: four of the most famous 100-mile trail races in the same year. Not content with four, she added a fifth, all of them coming within a 16-week period. She remains the oldest runner to have completed the Western States 100, the Leadville Trail 100, the Wasatch Front 100, the Old Dominion 100-Mile Trail Run, and the Angeles Crest 100.

Her favorite race, however, was one that she did not use as an opportunity to compete. Helen and her husband Norm, who when he has time to train is a very creditable ultrarunner, are co-race directors of the Western States 100.

In 1993, Norm's opportunities for training were rare. But that came as a mixed blessing. Helen and Norm signed up for a five-day 100-mile stage race in the shadows of the Himalayas, an area of the world to which they'd traveled before to hike to several of the Everest base camps, an area of the world both of them love.

With Norm's training in eclipse that year, Helen and he were at a similar level, so for the first time in years, they had the opportunity to run at roughly the same pace, enjoying the scenery, enjoying each other at a leisurely pace, enjoying the camaraderie of other runners on the trip. "It was marvelous," Helen recalls. "I wouldn't trade it for all the tea in India. It was a very special five days for Norm and me. We're both so busy. But this was an opportunity to run together through some of the most inspiring terrain on Earth and to slow down enough to be with each other every step of the way."

A friend of Helen's has recently put together a book of Helen's accomplishments and inspirational sayings, titled *No Limits Living*. For a copy, send $10 to:
  Helen Klein
  11139 Mace River Court
  Rancho Cordova, CA 95670

Experiencing more days when it is increasingly difficult to get yourself out the door to run isn't a sign that you no longer love running. Although if you let it go long enough, it could develop in that direction. It is merely human nature that we become bored (or at least less psyched) about that which has become habit.

Many mature runners have come back to running better by far by giving in to a serious bout of motivational meltdown. Sometimes we need a rest, both physically and mentally. Sometimes a running program can be revived by completely reorganizing both it and the running and racing goals. (See chapters 12–14 and 21–25.)

It isn't a matter that, like Alcoholics Anonymous, you need to get up in front of a group of fellow runners and say, "Hi. My name's Mike. And I feel I've let myself and all of you down because last Thursday I felt so unmotivated that I didn't do the five-miler I was scheduled to do. I read a magazine article instead." Hey, Mike, it ain't the end of the world. Beat yourself up too much over a lapse of motivation and more and more runs will become horrible chores until you eventually find all the joy gone from your running.

Not every run's going to be fun, an uplifting experience, an epiphany. You've run enough miles to know that. The secret is to accept the bad runs or the runs undone and not beat up on yourself over them. As with Bad Bod Syndrome, we'll discuss Bad Brain Disease a whole bunch more as we jog through this book.

Goaling

*"Whatever you can do,
or dream you can, begin it.
Boldness has genius, power,
and magic in it."*

—Goethe

"So how's your running going?"
"Oh, so-so . . .."
"You gonna run the 10K next week?"
"I dunno. Maybe. . . ."

It takes no genius to conclude that this is a running program spiraling downward.

It would be heaven if we could all run only when the spirit moves us and still run well whenever we want. But for most of us, that isn't how running—or life—works. Anything worthwhile requires an investment, whether it's an investment of time, money, emotional lucre, or spiritual specie. That which is attained too easily is worth about what it took to get it, which is why self-esteem cannot be bestowed, but must be earned.

Certainly, during periods of injury recovery and for at least one extended three- to four-week general recuperation period per year, it is advisable to run as we feel, if at all. But for a running program to be effective, for the runner to run well and be motivated to continue to do so, consistency and goal setting are essential.

There is a tendency, whether consciously or subconsciously, for some of the fire to go out of our running as we age and to realize, sometimes in truly dramatic fashion, that our fastest times are behind us. This is a natural and understandable reaction, more troublesome for some than for others, depending on how much of one's ego is invested in clocked performances.

In chapter 1 we discussed Bad Bod Syndrome and Bad Brain Disease, the two prime obstacles to fulfilled running beyond age 50. This is the time to guard against the dreaded Bad Brain Disease, that lethargic twilight zone where we run merely out of habit, and without the vigor and motivation we once enjoyed and would like to again attain.

We'll keep coming back to Bad Brain Disease in subsequent chapters until we've hammered it into submission. But a good method of starting to short-sheet Bad Brain Disease is to take a regularly-scheduled meeting with yourself for the purpose of setting short- and long-range goals.

Recall the palpable energy in the air in 1995 as literally tens of thousands of runners across the country and around the world worked themselves to a frenzy in an attempt to qualify for the "100th" running of the Boston Marathon. If we could have captured that electricity, we could have lighted a half-dozen major cities for a year. The excitement was generated by what those tens of thousands of runners saw as a worthy but difficult and possibly attainable goal: to line up in Hopkinton on April 15, 1996.

Setting New Goals

The vast majority of runners who've passed a 50th birthday have personalities that thrive on setting—and reaching—goals. How else does a runner successfully get 10, 15, 20 years of running under the waistband of those running shorts? The problem arises when we become so used to our daily run that we allow it to slip into habit. We consequently find ourselves setting goals half-heartedly—if at all.

I know that if I say, "Well, yeah, I think I want to run the Humboldt Redwoods Marathon this fall," my training and performance will be mediocre, if I line up at the starting line at all. But if I say, "Yeah! I wanna do a 3:30 at Humboldt," and then pull the calendar from the wall and begin crayoning in specific prime workouts toward that goal, it's gonna happen. There's a major difference in the two approaches. With no clearly defined goals laid out, there is no road map to lead you to them, and the tendency is to drift aimlessly through your running. This confers no great value to it so that it, in turn, has nothing substantial to return to you.

It's never too late—or too early—to set or reset short- and long-term goals. This process need not be complicated, but it must encompass years and years rather than mere weeks or months. I've always been impressed by Finland's legendary distance runner Lasse Viren. During the 1970s Viren was in possession of so much patience and held such long-term goals that rather than employing year-long running cycles, he created four-year cycles of peaking. The fourth year just happened to coincide with an Olympic year in which he developed the habit of winning the gold in both the 5,000- and 10,000-meter races. Relatively speaking, the three years between Olympics produced mediocre results and Viren just didn't care, because it was all part of his master plan.

Our long-term running goals need not be Olympian, but need to be ambitious enough that they present a challenge. If you've toyed with the idea of training for and running a marathon, this may well be the time to go for it. If you've run marathons but you feel your performances have not tapped your true potential, this may be the time to set a goal of running a truly top-drawer marathon. If you've harbored the secret desire to try an ultramarathon, you would not be alone; many mature runners graduate to ultras when their competitive days at shorter races are behind them; ultras are the ultimate patient-pacing challenge and are not designed for the young and reckless.

Adopting Unique Goals

It is impossible to address, in detail, the goals of every runner who reads this. Each runner brings to this discussion a unique running history and an equally unique lifestyle into which only certain goals can reasonably be inserted.

Considering that limitation, let's create a runner, Sidney Waller, who is in his 55th year of life, and whose running has lately lacked the zip it once did. We'll see where Sid might take his running over the next one, two, three, five, and 10 years. From Sid's case, you can extrapolate your own goals.

Sid works at a small Silicon Valley software engineering firm. He's worked there for 11 years, generally enjoys his work, plans to work until they throw him out. He makes good money and receives five weeks vacation per year. He's been married for 28 years, has two grown (and moved-away) children, likes to read thrillers and political science books, enjoys playing chess with several friends one night a week, and his pride and joy is a red '55 Chevy that he keeps garaged and works on lovingly.

His running history is typical. He first became involved in running in 1978 during the first Running Revolution. He loved it and probably ran way too much: raced almost every weekend, ran at least four marathons a year, but by the mid-'80s began to burn out, stopped running completely for two years, then restarted and lately has found his running has been . . . well . . . lackluster. He's running four sessions per week totaling 20–25 miles. He wants to recapture some of the excitement he enjoyed back in 1978.

Balancing Your Goals

The balancing act in setting running goals is to set goals ambitious enough that they offer a worthy challenge but not so difficult that they are practically unattainable. Toward that end, it is usually best to have one prime goal each year with several secondary or ongoing goals. Let's put together Sid's goals, with his prime goal for the year italicized, then take a look at his rationale.

Year 1:

Run 4–5 days per week.

Take time off from running between Thanksgiving and Christmas.

Run at least six 10Ks during the year.

Run a fall marathon in under four hours.

Year 2:

Run 4–5 days per week.

Take time off from running between Thanksgiving and Christmas.

Run four 10Ks during the year.

Run a spring marathon in under four hours.

Train for and run a fall 50-miler.

Year 3:

Run 4–5 days per week.

Take time off from running between Thanksgiving and Christmas.

Run one spring and one early-fall marathon, each under four hours.

Run a late-fall 50-miler.

Begin an upper body strengthening program.

Year 4:

Same as Year 3, with improved time goal in 50-miler.

Year 5:

Run 4–5 days per week; one of these is a track workout.

Take time off from running between Thanksgiving and Christmas.

Continue upper body strengthening program.

Run at least six 10Ks during the year.

Run one spring marathon.

Run a fall 50-miler.

On birthday, run a timed mile at the track.

Years 6–9:

Similar to Year 5, with work toward reasonable age-group performances in one 10K and one marathon.

Year 10:

Run 4–5 days per week; one of these is a track workout.

Take time off from running between Thanksgiving and Christmas.

Run one spring marathon and one fall ultra.

On birthday, run a timed mile at the track.

Run at least five 10Ks during the year.

Run an ultra adventure run.

The Rationale

What does Sid's program have going for it? Regularity, progressively more ambitious goals, planned rest periods, and running events with which he is already familiar mixed with running events he has not yet tried, including an adventure run.

Regularity

To be successful, a running program saturated with specific racing goals must be pursued on a regular, structured basis. For people involved in a running program, the structure of running four or five days a week makes the program comfortable for them because it is something on which they can count and it is something that—unlike much of the rest of the world—has predictable results.

Progressively More Ambitious Goals

To keep a set of goals lively, you need to continually raise the bar. In Sid's case, he has taken on challenges that are difficult but not impossible. He has not overdone his goal setting so that his entire year is filled with running and racing. Yet each year holds something new, whether it's his first ultra or for the first time in his life embarking on an upper body strengthening program, a program which will have marked benefits for his marathoning and ultrarunning.

Planned Rest Periods

I'm a staunch proponent of taking roughly a month off from running each year. This is especially important as we age. A regular running program produces microscopic muscle and tissue tears that are similar to a misty rain. Watch the little drops of water on the windshield of a car: they fall, they settle in, and little by little they shift, running together, until they form larger drops before sliding off the glass. The microscopic tears are not by themselves a problem, but if we allow them to build up, over time the little tears begin to interconnect, forming larger tears, until ultimately they form an injury. Give your body a month off from running and it will come back refreshed. Marshal Ulrich, a very accomplished ultrarunner from Colorado and course record-holder on the Death Valley-to-Mt. Whitney 150-mile ultramarathon course, takes one month off each year. He does no running during that period and invariably comes back stronger each January than he was the January before.

© Ken Lee

Mixed Running Challenges

Sid had run marathons during the 1970s and 1980s, so taking on the challenge of the marathon is not new; but what he adds to the marathon challenge is a specific time goal, in this case sub-4:00. Running a timed mile on his birthday is new for Sid. He's never raced the mile, but it adds a unique twist to his year in two ways: the mile is a new challenge requiring more speedwork—speedwork specific to his mile run challenge but that benefits him in his performances in the marathon and in his 50-miler.

The Adventure Run

This is a goal that can put an entirely new spin on an old running program (see chapter 25). An adventure run is an ultramarathon event that you put together as though you were a race director. It can be as simple as running a 30-mile segment of the Appalachian Trail, with friends meeting you at various junctures along the way to give you aid. Or it can be as ambitious as running across your home state, with friends providing a mobile aid station every several miles. In 1989 Tom Crawford and I became the first people to ever run from Badwater in Death Valley (the lowest point in the Western Hemisphere and hottest place on Earth) to the peak of Mt. Whitney (at 14,494 feet, the highest peak in the contiguous U.S.) and back to Badwater, a distance of 300 miles. We did it in midsummer and started at 6 A.M., both to enjoy the obscene heat of Death Valley and because the peak of Whitney is snow-covered in winter. The adventures we encountered along the way will be with us vividly the rest of our lives.

Sid's adventure run need not be as crazy as the Death Valley/Mt. Whitney out and back. But by putting together an adventure run of your own as a goal a decade down the road, each of your challenges along the way is a step toward that ultimate goal; each of the other challenges constitutes a link in the chain you're building toward your ultimate running adventure.

And what a goal it is! In a world of diminishing expectations and goals, your running program is driven for 10 years by an ultimate goal that will be the adventure of a lifetime.

PART

II

The Elements of Training

chapter

3

Enduring

*"The highest reward for a person's
toil is not what they get for it,
but what they become by it."*

—John Ruskin

Consistency is the backbone of any aerobic sports program. In order for an aerobic program to work, the activity must be done on a basis regular enough to allow it to build and maintain a foundation while it daily and weekly renews itself.

In other words, you run regularly to a certain level in order to keep yourself at that level of fitness, all other factors being equal. A runner who religiously puts in 25 miles per week will be able to continue to put in 25 miles a week indefinitely without a great deal of physical distress as long as everything else stays constant.

If you catch a cold and miss four days of running, your running will suffer, and when you come back you'll have to work harder to get back to the comfort zone of 25 miles per week. If you suffer an injury, say an Achilles tendon pull, you may miss three weeks of running. Coming back from a three-week layoff to get back to your usual 25 miles per week becomes something close to starting over.

It seems somehow unfair that it takes a good two months to get into half-decent aerobic condition but in only two weeks of layoffs, the conditioning can be significantly undermined. In that sense, fitness is hard work, but then, so is anything worth attaining.

On the flip side of the 25-miles-per-week comfort zone, if we gradually add to our weekly mileage by adding three to five miles every other week, we move out of our established comfort zone and little by little bump the comfort zone higher.

For many people who run, especially those in their 50s, 60s, 70s, and beyond, a program of running four or five days a week at a set mileage level is all they've ever done, all they want to do, all they'll ever do. For maintaining basic fitness, nothing could be simpler.

To Each His Own

To those runners who use the seasons of the year to dictate their cycles of training and who peak for various racing seasons, the idea of running 20 or 25 miles week-in and week-out, usually over the same courses, always at the same pace, appears to be the ultimate boredom. Yet if that's what is working for you and you're happy with it and you aren't becoming bored, more power to you.

I knew a woman in her mid-50s who worked herself up to the point where she ran 70 miles per week but never raced. I couldn't understand how she managed, for more than a dozen years, to maintain her program. She ran the same 10-mile course every weekday morning before going to work and she ran the same 10-mile course twice on Saturday, then took Sundays off. For more than 12 years, she maintained the same routine and for all I know she may still be doing it. When I asked her if she didn't get bored running the same course, she answered that her 10 miles was the only constant in her life, that it was the anchor she used to maintain her sanity. Her job in a hospital emergency room offered anything but consistency, and the problems she always seemed to be having with her two grown children only offered the consistency that whatever problems they had this week would be matched or surpassed next week.

This woman was a perfect example of establishing a base of endurance and then maintaining it. Almost to a fault. Fortunately, she ran so gently and was so biomechanically sound that the 10 miles a day never seemed to bother her. She even maintained that psychologically, the course was never exactly the same from one day to the next, and was therefore constantly fresh for her. Most runners are not nearly so serene in their running.

If we look at our running as a pyramid, with a yearly top-drawer competition or two serving as the peak of that pyramid, the endurance base is the foundation. For fitness runners, the foundation is all they're interested in. But for all runners, this foundation is where the entire program begins and ends. Without a good base, the more intense strengthening work and speedwork crumble.

Unfortunately, as we get more and more years of running under our running shorts, and as we age, we tend to ignore the simple beauty of formulating a program based upon those basic principles, and we tend to simply go out and run what we feel like, when we feel like it, or when we can fit it in.

This, of course, is not an across-the-board malady. Some runners sit down once a year and meticulously map out their upcoming year of training and racing like one of George Patton's armored campaigns. And frequently, these are the runners who are very successful and who stay motivated in their running. We can't expect to get more out of our running than we put into it, and some runners have programmed themselves to make their running the anchor of their lives.

Many of us, however, have slipped away from that commitment, and as a result our running has suffered. We would do well to borrow from the example of the successful runner and plan our running, especially the all-important endurance base, a year at a time.

Imitate Nature

Of course, the simplest format against which to place the endurance base work is nature itself, which involves following the seasons, something we tend to become more sensitive to the older we become. It is no accident that the two major marathon seasons each year are spring and fall. In the winter

it's generally too cold or cantankerous to race and in the summer it's generally too hot.

Keying our base endurance work to the seasons is about as basic as beginning running programs get, yet once our running program becomes second nature to us from years of practice, it is the basics that seem to fall through the cracks.

To ignore the hints that the seasons send us is to court disaster as far as our running goes. Consider, for example, the fact that Northern California is just about as ideal as it gets for running. Yet Northern California produces fewer world- and national-class runners than theoretically it should based upon the perfect training and racing conditions. Compare that to Lasse Viren coming out of Finland, one of the most abysmal of running environments, to win the 5,000 and 10,000 meters at the Olympics in 1972 and again in 1976. The problem with ideal running weather may simply be that runners tend to ignore the seasons and overtrain, running themselves into injury.

By annually restarting your endurance base after a rest period (see chapter 6) during the depth of winter, you can head off injuries by giving your muscles and tendons a vacation in which to heal, while also easing them back into service as winter wanes. The older we get, the more crucial this gentling process becomes.

The slow buildup of base mileage coming off the winter rest period should be as gentle as you can stand it while still cautiously increasing total mileage. This is a good period to work some walking into your training program. (We'll talk more about making good use of walking in chapter 8.)

Warm the Muscles First

When building your base mileage in late winter, it is a good idea to walk the first mile or so in order to warm the muscles and joints gently against the cold air before rolling into a jog. It is also a good idea in any weather, but especially in cold weather, to walk a mile or so *after* your running workout in order to cool and relax the legs back to normal. The hard-core runner will read this and begin muttering "Wimp! Wimp! Wimp!"

But to this day I remember a pleasant run that masters runner Mike Tymn and I took with Australian Albie Thomas two days before the 1978 Honolulu Marathon. Albie, then in his 40s, had run a 3:58.9 mile in Dublin on August 6, 1958, the fifth fastest time in a year when Herb Elliott set a world record of 3:54.5 in the same race. As we ran along a side street in Honolulu, chatting away, Albie ran off the street and off the sidewalk and onto every patch of dirt he could find. "I'm preservin' my legs," he said. "If ya wanna have a long running career, you've gotta go easy on your legs. And get plenty rest."

If a guy who was one of the pioneers in the world in breaking the four-minute mile, who'd managed to continue running well for decades, was advising us to go gently on our legs whenever the opportunity presented itself and to get plenty of rest, who was I to doubt?

And apply Albie Thomas' theories to your endurance runs: if you have a choice between running a concrete sidewalk or an asphalt bike path that parallels the road, always choose the asphalt; the asphalt is several times softer than the concrete. The same goes for dirt roads and trails: if they are available, always pick dirt over asphalt or concrete.

Mix Distances

We also need to remember that even though building a base should be done slowly and gently, it should not be done monotonously. The same hard/easy theories that apply to a week's worth of workouts in the peak of the racing season apply to building a base of endurance. If your goal is to run 20 miles per week during the first week of February, and you want to do it in five days, don't run four miles on each of those five days. Instead, run 3, 6, 3, 5, 3. Or 4, 3, 4, 3, 6. Anything but 4, 4, 4, 4, 4.

By using the hard/easy method in something even as basic as a 20-mile week, you head off boredom by using different courses. You also gradually build toward a longer run of six miles, a method you'll be incorporating as your mileage increases and your long runs need to be increased.

Consider Racing Workouts

For runners who never race, an entire new dimension can be added to your running program by adding even a handful of 5Ks and 10Ks to the prime (spring and fall) seasons. You don't necessarily need to build strength and speed. Do your regular base training and use that foundation from which to race. Run the first mile or two as you would your regular daily workouts, then as you warm up increase your speed by 15 seconds per mile.

Yours wouldn't be the first running program rejuvenated by moving up to racing. Of course, the process works in the other direction, also. The runner who has raced regularly for too many years can sometimes revive the legs and the spirit by canceling a season's worth of racing and instead running base mileage to give the body—and head—time to recuperate on deep levels.

The Matter of Footwear

Another frequently overlooked item in this area that can affect us negatively as we accumulate more and more mileage on our legs is the quality and condition of our running shoes. Don't be stingy in buying this essential piece of equipment; investing in a pair of good running shoes is almost always less expensive than paying a podiatrist or orthopedic surgeon to take care of the results of going too far in a worn-out pair.

The running shoe is, in essence and in fact, merely a portable cushioned platform upon which the runner can land safely. Early Boston marathoners ran in street shoes that they modified to remove some of the weight and stiffness. Some ran in track shoes with the spikes removed. Others had custom leather racing shoes made for them. Jim Peters, the Englishman who was the first runner to dip under 2:20 for the marathon, ran in what were known as plimsoles—lightweight white tennis-like recreation shoes that today a runner would consider cruel and unusual punishment.

Modern running shoes are light years ahead of what they were during the First Running Revolution in the mid-1970s. The technology of new materials that better absorb the shock of the foot contacting the running surface has advanced tremendously. Motion control devices have also advanced to the nearly-sublime.

When new to the sport of running, whether you're 50 or 65, begin your running shoe search with the most basic shoe you can find that addresses your needs, and increase the complexity of the shoe model from there as needed. Fortunately, most specialized running shoe stores have salespeople who are runners themselves and who are often obsessed with learning as much as they can about the shoes they sell. Be up-front with the shoe salesperson: shod me in the most basic, inexpensive shoe that will work for my particular biomechanical needs.

Take as much time shopping for and trying out various shoe models as you would shopping for a new car. After all, these are your feet, ankles, legs, knees, and hips we're trying to protect. Most good running shoe stores will allow you to try on the shoes and then run around the block in them to get a better feel for whether or not they'll work. Of course, with some models, it takes a few miles on the road before incompatibilities surface.

What we need to realize as we shop for shoes is that the 50+ runner typically has more complex shoe needs than his or her nieces or nephews if for no other reason than the fact that over the years, feet change in response to doing all that work of holding the body up against the forces of gravity that are beating down upon them. The feet may have also been the victim of years of "pedabuse." This is a term I use for the torture some people put their poor feet through. More a female than male deviation, foot problems are fairly common among 50+ women because much of their youth was spent striving to adhere to the whims of fashion. Read that as two cardinal sins against the feet: squeezing feet into shoes too small to comfortably accommodate them and wearing high heels.

The technological advances of the basic running shoe and the tossing away of the chains of foot fashion are responsible for the huge influx of elderly nonrunners wearing running shoes. Compared to what they've worn all their lives, running shoes are like clouds for the feet.

Too many people run in their current favorite model of running shoe, walk in the door, and throw them in a corner—even if those faithful shoes have just carried them through five miles of rain- and mud-spattered road. For the longevity of your feet, ankles, legs, and knees, your running shoes should be properly maintained. You should also have several pairs being broken in at the same time so that you can alternate pairs of shoes. Alternating running shoes provides a giant step toward minimizing the chance of injury from overuse through the repeated striking of the foot upon the running surface at exactly the same angle over and over and over.

Monitor the health of your shoes. If they are broken down, if the heel is worn down to the midsole, if the compression of the sole seems compromised, invest in a new pair of shoes. There is a tendency among older runners to be conservative in their buying habits. Your running shoe is not the place to be fiscally conservative. Replace them as needed. When you find a model that is particularly good for you, stockpile them because it's an immutable law of running that as soon as you find the perfect running shoe, it will be discontinued. Running is a relatively cheap sport compared to most. The running shoe is the only major expense, and for your continued comfort and injury-free running, keep yourself well shod.

There is no phase of your running (endurance base, strength work, speedwork) where you can afford running on broken-down or inferior shoes. You don't need to buy the most expensive, you merely need to buy the model that is best for your biomechanics. And just as you alternate your courses in your endurance base buildup, alternate your shoes. In conclusion, don't beat your feet. Buy them the good shoes they need. If you don't, trust me, they'll let you know you've done them dirt.

THE HIGH-TECH WORLD

Running shoes have become so high-tech and sophisticated in design and materials that it is very easy for the average runner to become overwhelmed when visiting a running shoe store to buy a new pair of shoes. This is especially true for the more mature runner who has not necessarily been inclined to assiduously follow the technical advances and who is looking for what amounts to a good, modestly-priced, functional running shoe.

Not to fear. Just because the shoes have lots of bells and whistles and enough loud colors to overwhelm even an interior decorator doesn't mean you need to cower in front of the wall displays. And there is no need to blow the budget buying shoes that feature expensive—but often unnecessary—features.

The best advice when contemplating buying a new pair of running shoes is to do some research first. Both of the major running magazines, *Runner's World* and *Running Times*, do a fine job of evaluating new models and explaining improvements in running shoe technology. It is worth pulling out the latest running shoe evaluation issue and becoming familiar with the terms used to describe various features in running shoes. The magazines usually provide the basics of a running shoe and then go off into explanations of various applications that address specific biomechanical or body weight considerations. It is logical, for instance, that a 135-pound male's impact protection needs would be somewhat less weighty than that of a 205-pounder.

It is important to know something about the basics of running shoes. And the most basic of the basics is that there are typically three layers to the soles: inner, midsole, and outer. All three layers wear in their own particular way.

The outer sole, that which comes in contact with the ground and is usually made of rubber, wears by the rubber being scuffed off through repeated contact with the surface; the wear typically comes at the heel. The midsole is worn by becoming compressed by the weight of the runner's body repeatedly landing on the midsole, whose job it is to absorb that weight as best it can. Repeated use gradually compresses the midsole material until its ability to absorb shock is compromised. The inner sole is worn more gradually, by the impact and friction of the foot upon the light cushioning and stabilizing material forming the contact between the foot's (or sock's) sole and the shoe.

Most of the high-tech impact-absorbing modules (air, gel, etc.) are merely variations on a theme: How do we better dampen the foot's impact with the earth?

Practical Points

There are some practical points to keep in mind when hunting for and using running shoes:

1. Shop at a reputable running shoe store. You may pay a few bucks more than at a discount shoe store, but the service you receive in exchange is well worth the money. Be prepared to spend at least a half-hour trying on various models suggested by the salesperson based upon what you tell him or her about your running habits and biomechanical peculiarities. Always bring a pair of your used running shoes with you so the salesperson can "read" the wear characteristics. By reading the wear of your used shoes, the salesperson can often make more astute recommendations for your new shoes.

2. If you wear any orthotics or over-the-counter lifts or other appliances inside your shoes to accommodate your feet, bring the device along so you can try the new shoe with the appliance in place and so the salesperson can make certain you are trying on a shoe size that has the extra space to accommodate the device.

3. Always buy shoes a bit larger than snug. You want roughly a half-inch of dead air space in the toebox in front of your longest toe. This is for two reasons: on the downhills, your foot will slide

forward, and you want some space for the toes so they don't strike the front inside of the shoe, and if you do long runs, after the first hour of running, the feet tend to swell and expand and the expansion needs space to be comfortably accommodated. If you don't provide the extra space in the toebox, the toes will become bruised and/or blistered.

4. Always keep several pairs of shoes in service at any given time, rotating through the several pairs, in order to impact at slightly different angles so that you do not cause overuse injuries. This is especially important for older runners, who are more prone to overuse injuries simply because they do not recuperate from workouts as quickly as young runners.

5. When you find a shoe model that is right for you, spend a few bucks and stockpile a few extra pairs, because no sooner will you and your feet fall in love with that model than it will disappear. Stay current with your salesperson as to the status of the model of shoe you find works for you; the salespeople interact with the shoe company reps all the time and often have advanced warning when a specific model is going to be discontinued. They can be your early-warning system as to when it is time to stockpile. Also check back once word gets out that your favorite model is going to be discontinued because once the decision is made, the shoe company will often discount the model in order to empty its warehouse stock. The shoe company's discounting is a real savings to you and a further incentive to stockpile.

6. Take care of your shoes. If you run trails and your shoes get crusted with dirt and mud, periodically clean them. Don't put them in a clothes dryer to dry them, however. Stuff the wet shoes with newspaper (to absorb some of the dampness) and lay them on their sides to dry in a warm (but not hot) place. This is also true for shoes that are worn during a workout in rainy weather. This is an additional reason to keep several pairs of shoes in circulation at any one time. You won't feel compelled to quick-dry your running shoes, which tends to break them down faster.

7. Monitor the wear of your shoes. It is incredible how many runners gauge the usable life remaining in their running shoes by the condition of the uppers (everything from the insole up). The uppers have nothing to do with the remaining life in a pair of running shoes. Two other factors are more important: the compression of the absorption material in the midsole and the wear of the outersole. When the outersole wears down through the rubber and into the midsole, the shoe is telling you it needs to be put to rest. The compression of the insole is a little more difficult to gauge, but by paying attention to how "hard" the shoe seems to be getting you should be able to tell when it has run past its "useful" life. How long does a good pair of shoes usually last?

There are a lot of factors involved, including your body weight, the kind of running you do, the model of shoe, and so on. But on average, a pair of running shoes should last about 500 miles.

chapter 4

Strengthening

"Success doesn't come to you . . .
you go to it."

—Marva Collins

There is a myth in America that is only gradually being debunked. That myth holds that as we age we become weaklings and should therefore be protected from ourselves for our own good.

The myth is based in the belief that people over 50 suddenly become fragile porcelain things poised to break at the first possible encounter with a real-life obstacle. This perceived fragility covers both the physical and mental. Have you ever heard a well-meaning but muddleheaded grown child say to a parent, "Now don't you worry your little self about it. We'll take care of it."?

We then wonder why so many older people can no longer take care of themselves. They simply aren't encouraged to do so and therefore end up buying into the myth that as we age we reach a point where we literally drop off the edge of a cliff in both our physical and mental capacity:

Yeah, the Old Man's been changing his own oil since he rebuilt his first car at 18, but now that he's turned 60 we've convinced him to have someone else do it for him.

We finally brought Grandma to her senses. Playing bingo until 10:30 at night. . . . At her age. . . .

The fact is that no matter your age, your muscles are eagerly waiting to do something good for you. The muscles aren't programmed to atrophy; they're programmed to build strength from meeting resistance.

One of my favorite research projects involved old, seemingly atrophied muscles. Dr. Peter Wood, who until his recent retirement was the associate director of the Stanford (University) Center for Research in Disease Prevention in Palo Alto, California, summarized a study in his 1992 report on "Aging: Don't Take It Sitting Down!" in the *Encyclopedia Britannica Medical and Health Annual:*

> *Loss of muscle protein typically occurs with aging and can be very pronounced in people aged 80 and beyond. Yet in active old people, muscle mass seems to be relatively preserved. In an important recent study by Maria A. Fiatarone, William J. Evans, and colleagues from the U.S. Department of Agriculture Human Nutrition Research Center on Aging at Tufts University in Boston, 10 frail, institutionalized men and women, averaging 90 years of age, took part in an eight-week program of high-intensity resistance training of the leg muscles. Strength increased by 174%; muscle area, measured by a computed tomography (CT) scan, increased 9%; and mobility substantially improved. Two participants who had previously relied on canes for walking were able to dispense with them after the training program. Strength training has also been shown to reduce the frequency of falls and consequent fractures that are common in older persons owing to muscle decline and weakness in the lower extremities.*

Upper Body Strength

Fortunately, relative to most of the population, runners of any age have a fair amount of strength in their lower extremities as a result of their ongoing endurance program. Unfortunately, runners of all ages seldom have strength in other muscle groups, especially those in the upper body. In this chapter, we'll consider both the benefits that come from building strength in the abdominals and arms and back, and then we'll consider the benefits to your overall running program that can result from layering strength workouts over your aerobic endurance base.

It's the rare runner of any age who takes the trouble to build any muscle groups beyond the legs. Yet one's running can improve significantly by regularly incorporating a series of simple upper body strengthening exercises into their routine. The object, of course, is not to build bulk, since bulk involves extra weight, and a runner does not need to carry around extra weight. The object is to build strength and endurance into the arms and shoulders, and strength into the abdominals and back muscles.

In the late 1970s, Dr. Peter Cavanagh, who researches biomechanics at Penn State University, found that a runner's efficiency can be increased by nearly 12 percent by proper use of the arms. Unfortunately for the average runner, the longer the run or race, the more tired the arms become. And the arms are important to maintaining an efficient running stride because they work like metronomes, rhythmically pacing the legs. In the latter stages of a long run or race, the legs will naturally tire and the stride and/or leg speed slows. This process is aggravated by the arms tiring.

The Resistance Movement

Resistance exercises to strengthen the arms can be as simple as using a piece of firewood to do arm curls, gradually increasing the number of repetitions as your strength grows. But always use a piece of firewood or hand weights small enough to offer some resistance but not so much that you begin to build bulk. You can work a series of simple arm curls into a post-run strengthening workout that would also include simple push-ups.

Push-ups done slowly and with an eye toward holding good form strengthen the back, the arms, and the shoulders, all of which play a significant role in the latter stages of a long run or race. You don't need to do a great number of push-ups; start with four or five. Add more as your strength grows. The beauty of push-ups is that your own body provides the resistance; you don't need to invest in any equipment.

The other important muscles in your running program are the abdominals. Weak, flabby abdominals cause a runner to cave in on him- or herself in the latter stages of a long run or race, which in turn shortens the stride and closes down the chest cavity, thereby restricting the amount of air you can deliver to the lungs. Additionally, weak abdominals, being the opposing muscles to the lower back, can contribute to lower back problems. The solution is a regular program of sit-ups. Not exaggerated sit-ups; merely simple, short-ranged crunches that are easy on the back muscles and that flex and tone the abdominals.

The simplest way to work these basic upper body strengthening exercises into your regular running routine is to do them as a part of your cool-down following your weekday runs. Perhaps start by doing 10 sit-ups, 5 push-ups, and 20 arm curls. In two weeks, move up to 12 sit-ups, 6 push-ups, and 24 arm curls.

Besides improving your running posture, the upper body exercises will help you defy the gravity that seems to draw older people toward the ground until they walk around looking like question marks.

Strengthening Your Run

As far as strengthening your running goes, once you have the aerobic endurance base established, the single simplest way to add strength to your stride is by running hills. If you've never used hill running as a strengthening tool, you've got something to look forward to because a regular program of hill running will do wonders for your regular running and especially for your racing.

Some runners avoid hills the way they avoid the track, while others take to the hills as though they were addicted to them. Runners who regularly run hills are regularly better runners because the hills build strength into the upper legs. The strength built into the legs from running hills isn't merely effective in running hills—it also translates to more powerful running on the flat. This is especially effective for older runners, who need to make use of everything they can squeeze

into their bag of tricks if they're going to be competitive against the younger crowd.

When runners avoid hill workouts it is usually because they fear them. The fear comes either from fear of the workouts hurting or fear of injury from doing such strenuous workouts, or fear on both counts.

Start Slowly

Banish both fears. First of all, you don't have to run up the side of a steep mountain to do a hill workout. In fact, it is better if you don't. If you run hills that are too steep, the only thing you train yourself for is running steep hills. And second of all, you are much more likely to injure yourself running downhill than uphill simply because you are increasing the impact to your feet, ankles, knees, and legs when you run downhill (on the order of four to five times your body weight), while you are lessening that impact when you run uphill, in the process strengthening your thighs and stretching your Achilles tendons.

As we older runners age, we lose muscle strength and need to constantly rebuild it. Age also brings on a tightening of the tendons. The more we can regularly loosen the tendons, the healthier they will be. This is especially true of a tendon like the Achilles, which is so important to the good biomechanics of running.

The Achilles tendon is the usually taut tendon that connects the top of the heel to the bottom of the calf. Because it is a tendon, and a large one at that, its blood supply is limited. Because the blood supply is limited, the system is not very efficient at carrying away injured cells, which makes the Achilles tendon very slow to heal. Yet the Achilles is extremely important to running, as it supplies much of the springing motion we release when we toe off.

Famed podiatrist John Pagliano reports that mature runners develop more lower back and Achilles tendon pain than their younger counterparts. Both tend to suffer from overuse as we age, whether or not we run.

For a healthy Achilles, warm up slowly before picking up your pace. And pay attention to wear patterns on the heels of your running shoes: the more wear, the more stress is placed on the Achilles tendon. Warm the Achilles up on the flats or downhills before tackling a hill, which tends to overextend the Achilles.

Hill running should be done only after you warm up by jogging through a couple of miles. Hill running should not be done on a steep hill. The ideal hill is one that is about a quarter-mile long and whose angle is only a few degrees—just enough to make you work but not strain. You do not need to charge the hills to effectively strengthen your legs. Keep the same cadence as you use in regular running on the flats, but shorten your stride to downshift for the hill.

As with any other series of workouts, begin by doing the hill once. The following week, try it twice. Begin working the hills into your weekly training roughly 8 to 10 weeks before you plan to begin your racing season. Do the hill repeats once or twice a week, working them into the mid-portion of a regularly scheduled medium-length workout.

It is truly impressive to watch a runner who enjoys running hills. Dick Collins of Oakland, California was a runner in his 60s who ran hundreds of marathons and ultramarathons. He loved to run trails, which usually come equipped with a good share of hills. The magnificent thing about Dick was that although he was not a particularly fast runner, when he reached a hill, he powered up it as though he were a locomotive, actually running almost the same speed uphill as he ran on the flats. The hills were also where Dick passed other runners.

DICK COLLINS

When he was 41 years old, Dick Collins decided to change his life. The head of a major construction company in San Francisco, Dick led a high-pressured life. He smoked, he was overweight by more than 60 pounds, he was on a course for the classic American collision with an early death.

His doctor told him he'd better improve his diet and begin getting some exercise—or else. Dick took a good, long look at himself and acknowledged that what his doctor told him was right. "I was in the same stage a lot of people went through," Dick said. "Not in very good condition and heavy. The unhealthy aspects were getting to me. My doctor wanted to start giving me EKGs just to have a baseline because he figured down the line I'd be having a heart attack."

That was 1975. Dick began running—before he quit smoking. Then he began dieting. "The diet and the running kind of went together; then the weight came off pretty easy," he said in a November 3, 1986 interview with the *San Francisco Chronicle* a few days before he was to run his one hundredth ultramarathon. To that point he had gone from being an overweight smoker to running 99 races of 30 miles or above without ever dropping out of one.

Although not fast, Dick was determined and in ultramarathons, determination often pays off. He'd won the July 1984 Gator 24-Hour Race in San Francisco, with a total of 116 miles. In March of 1985 he'd set an American record for 52-year-olds in a Santa Rosa 24-hour race with 111-1/2 miles.

At 5'11" and roughly 180 pounds in racing trim, Dick was not the classic lithe distance runner. Like many an ultrarunner, he was built more for endurance than for speed. His steady shuffling seemed to never vary, whether he was running on the flats or going uphill. He referred to himself as The Rhino. Others referred to him as The Locomotive.

As hard-edged and wired as he was at his job, he was just the opposite in his dealings with fellow runners. He was soft-spoken, gentle, supportive, a friend to all.

He was also as active on the organizational side of the sport as he was on the running side. He was instrumental in creating the famed Quadruple Dipsea, the Quicksilver 50, and Ohlone Wilderness 50K. He also directed two fine ultradistance races himself, the Ruth Anderson 100K (named after his training partner and one of the most famous female ultrarunners) and the Firetrails 50-Miler.

In all, he ran more than 800 races without dropping out of one. When the drop finally came, at the Leadville Trail 100-Mile race in Colorado in August of 1988, Dick took it all philosophically: "Ya know," he said, "it wasn't so bad dropping out. If I'd have known it wasn't so bad, I'd have dropped out of races long ago."

Dick died of a heart attack on February 18, 1997 at the age of 63 while watching the Eco-Challenge multi-day event on television. He'd be the first to contend that he'd lived longer—and better—than he'd ever imagined he would when his doctor confronted him about his bad habits back in 1975. In all, Dick Collins completed more than 1,000 races, more than 250 of them beyond 30 miles.

Not bad for a rhino.

Of course, in a race, if a hill is steep enough that you can walk it as fast as you can run it, it's best to walk it. Doing so saves your legs by using them differently than the running motion does, thereby in effect massaging them a bit before they next roll into their running stride.

Much of your approach to hills involves not only shifting gears in your legs, but shifting gears in your head. Learn to take hills for what they are: a golden opportunity to strengthen your legs and improve your running program. Every once in a while you run into someone who hated hills with a passion until they gradually worked them into their program. Now you literally can't keep them out of the hills. They've obviously found a secret they want to use to its maximum. It puts them a leg up on the competition, and can do the same for you.

Speeding

"Nothing happens by itself. . . .
It all will come your way, once
you understand that you have
to make it come your way,
by your own exertions."

—Ben Stein

Speed kills. That's the conventional wisdom when applied to drugs and automobiles. When applied to automobiles an argument could be made that the theory is incorrect, considering that 85 percent of auto accidents are caused not by speed but by inattention.

As far as running goes, and especially as far as running for the older runner goes, speed doesn't kill. It thrills, as long as you can manage to work your way through the massive emotional minefield of negative images we have all stored up about speed workouts.

There is nothing so exhilarating, so preternaturally satisfying, as to run fast: that feeling of your body in full realization of its intrinsic design, the feel of a breeze moving past your face (a breeze that *you* are creating by moving through the air), the sudden shift of the arms and legs into a synchronized symphony of movement that is absent from the simple and crude jostling act of jogging. For a moment, or for a few moments, you become the Concorde supersonic jetliner over the Atlantic, not the Concorde with its snout aimed toward the ground sitting at a terminal.

And literally anyone can do speed—at least for a short distance. A sedentary person can run at full tilt for a half-block in pursuit of a vanishing bus and in the process can feel the thrill of rapid movement.

For the runner, there are a number of ways to do speedwork: go to the track and do repetitions at various shorter distances, engage in fartlek (Swedish for "speed play") workouts, run fast downhill, or enter races.

Unfortunately, most runners avoid the track with the same avidity they avoid the IRS, and for good reason. Too many of us have been ruined for the track by gym teachers or misled track coaches who functioned under the philosophy that if you weren't throwing up after a track workout, you hadn't worked hard enough.

Speed workouts, especially those at the track, should not be gut-wrenching exercises in masochism. Track workouts should be used to gradually (and painlessly) increase leg speed and stride. The important word there is *gradually*. Speed workouts on the track are also extremely important for developing a sense of pacing on a strictly-measured course and provide an opportunity to work on improving running form.

As mature runners, we must also overcome the stereotyped supposition that speedwork is safe only for the young, that older runners will hurt themselves by running fast. Speedwork is for everyone; it is especially useful for the older runner because it can be a wonderful tool for maintaining good biomechanics while increasing efficiency of gait, both of which gradually diminish as we age.

Arthur Lydiard, the fabled New Zealand coach, puts the goal of track workouts succinctly: "Initially, track training, other than sprint training, should not be at full speed. Rather, the tempo should be held back a little so that it can be raised as you progress. Speed should always be controlled, or you'll lose control of racing form later."

Speedwork is also important for older runners who are new to the sport and lifestyle. Too many mature but neophyte runners assume that all they are fit for is to jog at the same 10-minute-per-mile pace day after day, no matter what the distance of the workout or the race. Not true.

Speed can be increased three ways:

1. Increase leg speed.
2. Lengthen stride.
3. Combine 1 and 2.

Number 1 is preferable over number 2. A change in stride length can cause overstriding which, in turn, can cause biomechanical problems and injuries. An increase in leg speed (sometimes referred to as "leg turnover"), on the other hand, merely causes an increase in speed.

At the Track

Most road runners go out of their way to avoid the track. They'll go so far as to take a sizable detour if one of their daily workouts approaches a track.

When I worked at *Runner's World,* the staff had favorite running photos hung literally everywhere. One of the staff had a fairly perverted sense of humor. The half-dozen photos he hung were from the far side: a skeleton wearing running shoes and a singlet in full running stride with the headline "Run for Weight Loss," two guys dashing for a finish line wearing grimaces that made a shriveled Halloween pumpkin look good with the headline "Run for Fun," and so on. But my favorite of his ghoulish gallery was one of a college track runner limply holding himself over a trash bucket while retching, with a headline of "Speedwork Takes Guts."

For most runners, that photo and headline pretty much sum up track workouts. Each spring as we put together our Corporate Cup team we would literally have to kidnap people to get them to go to the track on Thursday evenings for team speed workouts. Yet, once we got them there, they enjoyed the workouts. Simply because the workouts were nothing like they'd experienced in the past. There were no gut-wrenching wind sprints. There was no hanging over the bucket puking. There was merely a gentle, gradual increase in speed done over shorter distances than we usually ran.

As the season progressed, our progress was significant. And of course the leg speed we'd built at the track translated to our daily workouts on the road as well as to our races both on the track and on the roads.

The secret to learning to tolerate—even enjoy—the track is twofold: make it fun, and don't run too fast too soon. If you are capable of running a 9:00 pace during your regular road workouts, your track repetitions need be nothing more exhaustive than repeating 400 meters in two minutes with a jogged lap between each or doing mile repeats at 8:30 with a walked lap between. You don't need to run 70-second laps or 7:00 miles—at least not yet. But by carefully and gradually lowering your times, you may well be able to reach times you thought impossible or that you haven't seen in 15 years. Aging robs us of speed very, very gradually. It doesn't undermine our speed overnight.

For those who've never engaged in speedwork, they have something marvelous to which they can look forward: major improvement in all phases of their running with the minor investment of one track session per week. It is astonishing how seductive running faster can be to a runner (of any age) who has not previously tapped into it. A fair number of the world's best veteran (read that "older") runners didn't begin running until later in life and afterwards found only by accident that they possessed natural speed they knew nothing about because they had never tapped into it.

What's the best way to ease into track workouts? Schedule them one day a week. And, if possible, invite someone of ability similar to yours to join you. Or put a little track group together and go out for pizza, beer, and a bull session afterwards. Make it as much fun as you can stand.

On your first session, warm up by jogging a mile or two; then, at your usual training speed, run a mile on the track, timing yourself. That time serves as your baseline. Walk a lap while you do the math.

Let's say your timed mile was 9:00. For your first speed workout, shoot to knock off 30 seconds. An 8:30 mile breaks down to four laps at roughly 2:07. Mark a spot on the track by placing a rock or your sweatshirt or something. Start your watch as you roll into a run. Check your watch as you come by the marked point on the track. More likely than not, due to anxiety, you'll be under your target 2:07. If you are, make an adjustment on your second lap to attempt to go past your marked spot at 4:14. Concentrate on keeping your form perfect and stay in control of your breathing. If you want, you can pick up the pace a little bit during the last lap's last straightaway. Click your stopwatch. Probably 8:25 or thereabouts.

Now, walk another lap to get your breathing back under control, and do another four laps at 2:07 each. When you're finished with your second mile, jog a mile to cool down, then go have your pizza and beer. Your first track workout is over. Nothing really terrible, was it?

Each week, you can alternate by increasing repeats or speed. For the second week, run three repeat miles at 8:30 pace. For the third week, run three repeat miles at 8:20 pace. For the fourth week, try four repeat miles at 8:20. And for the fifth week, try three repeat miles at 8:30 as a "rest" week. Play with gradually bringing the time down and the number of repeats up. But remember that the key word there is "gradually." Stay within your growing abilities. Don't make the workouts painful or boring.

Try variations. One of our favorites was doing pyramids. Do one lap at speed, jog a lap, do two laps at speed, jog a lap, do three laps at speed, jog a lap, do two laps at speed, jog a lap, do one lap at speed, then jog a lap. If you can entice your running friends to do the workouts with you, take turns pacing each other on mile repeats. As you become more experienced, play with predicting your pace by running a mile with a goal in mind but without looking at your watch until you cross the finish line. For another variation, if there is no one else at the track whom you'd impede, try running the laps clockwise instead of counterclockwise.

As you become more experienced, you can begin playing around with 100-meter or 100-yard sprints, but not at gut-wrenching speed. Use the sprints to increase your leg speed and also to practice your form and to more thoroughly integrate your arm swings into the power of your leg lifts.

There is no intrinsic evil in a track. There need be no great pain lurking there. It is available as one of the best tools a mature runner can use to improve pacing, increase leg speed, practice form, build confidence, make friends, and become a more relaxed running animal.

On the Fartlek Trail

The term "fartlek" translates from the Swedish as "speed play." Fartlek also translates to one of the most benign of all speed workouts because it involves painlessly mixing relatively mild speed in with your daily workouts.

Most runners do not regularly, consciously engage in fartlek running because most runners, especially older runners, do not have the luxury of having coaches to lead them through specific workout regimens. But most of us have probably been doing fartlek workouts without realizing it. You're out on a five-

© Terry Wild Studio

mile course you use maybe once a week. After two miles, you've begun to warm up and you hit a section of the course which is one of those psychologically uplifting stretches. You know those sections, where the spirit lifts a bit and the running becomes smoother, as opposed to the two-mile section in the regular six-mile course that runs past the landfill where the road is narrow and the hormonal-ravaged teenagers attempt to run anything on two or four feet off the road.

You go into this particularly positive mile stretch and you find yourself running how you feel, which in this case means picking up the pace, going to the arms a bit more strongly, paying attention to form. At the end of this golden mile, your run reverts to its normalcy: your speed moderates, your style goes back to what passes for normal, your run resumes its familiarity.

For that mile segment, you were playing with speed; you were engaged in fartlek. Fartlek is simply throwing in surges of speed in the middle of your regular run. It can be between telephone poles, it can be from one intersection to the next, it can be between mile posts along a highway, it can be that stretch that goes past the haphazardly chained junkyard dog.

For the sake of injury prevention, you wouldn't want to turn every one of your runs into a fartlek workout. But once or twice a week a bit of fartlek can bring your leg speed along very nicely, which in turn translates into generally better, faster runs even on your slow workouts.

Fartlek is also fun when done in a small group. Run with your friends, pick out a distant object (a fire hydrant, a particularly ugly car) and pick up your pace as you run toward it.

For the older runner who wants to build a little speed as humanely as possible, fartlek is the answer. And don't be bashful about taking advantage of your sudden knowledge of a foreign word. Work it into your daily conversation and see what kind of response it receives.

Going Downhill Fast

Another method of increasing stride and leg speed is to pick up the speed on downhill portions of courses or to schedule repeat downhill running once a week the way you would schedule uphill running in order to build strength. In fact, the downhill speed workouts could be done on the same stretch of road you have been using for your repeat hill workouts—but in the opposite direction.

The tendency among most runners is to approach downhill running cautiously, and for good reason. Other than tripping over exposed roots on running trails or being hit by inattentive drivers along well-traveled roads, there is probably no easier way to injure yourself running than running downhill badly. Downhill running, by the very physics of gravity, involves the body weight of the runner being multiplied three or four or even five times, which involves tremendous impact upon the feet, ankles, legs, and knees.

In downhill running, the tendency for most of us—especially if the downhill is particularly steep—is to use our legs to brake ourselves from going too fast. The braking action, unfortunately, aggravates the impact upon the feet, ankles, legs, and knees. The ideal downhill running involves leaning forward (against all your instincts) so that you are running perpendicular to the road surface. This provides for the smoothest downhill running, and the least wear and tear.

There are precious few excellent downhill runners. Bill Rodgers is one of them, which is one of the reasons he did so well at Boston, which is very much an overall downhill course. The first time Grete Waitz ran Boston, she dropped out at 20 miles with leg spasms because she had not practiced downhill running. She assumed you didn't need to do that.

Fortunately, the very act of running does much to strengthen bones, especially in older runners, so we come to the downhills with more going for us than the average sedentary individual who sits around losing bone density. Research at Stanford University proved that older people who run significantly increase their bone density over those who do not exercise and those who take part in nonimpact exercise. So the next time some sedentary person tries to tell you that running at your age will cause bone problems, you can rest assured the facts prove just the opposite.

Any downhill running for the purpose of speed should be done on a gentle downhill course. As in (up)hill running, the grade should be very gentle, in the area of 2 percent. Your downhill running for speed should also be done as smoothly as possible in regard to style. Concentrate on precise footplant and good form, keep the entire process under control, lean a bit forward into the downhill. And if you can find a downhill course that is on grass or dirt rather than asphalt or concrete, use it.

For runners over 50, downhill running for speed should be done sparingly unless you can find a forgiving grass or dirt surface. Once a week is plenty.

Off to the Races

The easiest—and for some the most pleasant—form of speedwork is to enter road races on a regular basis. Although some 50+ runners enter road races and jog through them seemingly at the same speed they do their weekday workouts, the very nature of a race entices a bit of speed out of even the most casual racer. Lining up with a few hundred or a few thousand other runners gets the adrenaline pumping and when the gun goes off, the urge to pick up the pace is almost built into us.

There are a fair number of older runners who run purely for the sake of running or for running's health benefits but who never, ever race. Entering the occasional road race is one way for 50+ runners to keep their interest in running alive and vital. It is also a good way of sneaking in your speed workout each week. And like many a 50+ runner before you who never raced and then tried it later in life only to learn they were very good at it, it can be very rewarding. Many an older runner has taken home a medal in age-group competition that was never anticipated when the entry form was filled out (see the profile of John Keston).

JOHN KESTON

Retirement to some means sleeping in, puttering around the house, and taking naps. For 72-year-old John Keston, it translates to running more than 60 miles a week toward his pursuit of world age-group records—between balancing his new career in virtual reality. Already the oldest runner in history to break three hours for the marathon (2:58:32 a few weeks before his 70th birthday), John broke the world record for the 70–74 age group (3:01:14) with a 3:00:58 marathon at the Twin Cities Marathon in late 1996.

Like many outstanding age-group runners, John Keston came to running later in life. While living in England, in order to be able to play demanding roles on the stage and screen he kept in shape by playing squash. He toured the U.S. with the Royal Shakespeare Company in 1975, which, in a very roundabout way, led him to living in America—and into running.

John was a professional actor and singer, the veteran of London theater, and a sought-after actor for international touring companies. An American friend who was visiting John one day asked him if he'd be interested in taking a position as artist-in-residence at Bemidji State University in northern Minnesota. While on an American tour with the Royal Shakespeare Company (which was presenting *Sherlock Holmes*), John visited Bemidji and decided to give teaching a try for one year. He ended up staying 20.

Fortunately for John and for the sport of running, Bemidji is not a hotbed of squash, so he took up running instead. In his first 10K race he ran 44:44 and won his age group. The heady feeling of performing on the roads as he did on stage motivated John to shoehorn his training into an already-busy schedule of building a fledgling performance arts department while also acting in various local and regional productions.

At the age of 63 John uncorked a startling 37:42 10K. He consistently ran sub-3:00 marathons up to nearly 70 years of age. Soon after turning 70, he established an age-group world record for the half marathon with a time of 1:24:05, beating the existing record by a full 51 seconds.

In 1995 he won both the 5,000 and 10,000 at the World Veterans Games in Buffalo. After retiring from teaching, John and his wife Anne moved to Oregon, and during the same summer, at the Oregon State Games, he set another age-group world record with a 5:34 mile. The performance earned him recognition as, from among some 17,000 participants, Oregon's outstanding athlete for 1995. Four weeks later he ran a new world record at 3,000 meters with a 10:51. Also in 1995 he returned to race in his native England for the first time. He ran a 3:01:35 at the London Marathon.

Since then John's goal has been to be the first runner over 70 to break three hours in the marathon. He repeatedly came close in 1996, with his 3:00:58 at Twin Cities capping a year in which he ran six marathons under 3:10.

In mid-1997, at the Hayward Field Masters' Classic in Eugene, Oregon, John set a world age-group record for 70- to 74-year-olds of 5:51.44 for the mile. He also set a single-age record for the 5,000 meters of 19:26:98. The previous month he had run a half marathon as training in 1:30:40, six days later running a 3:08:01 marathon at Grandma's Marathon in Duluth in 98 percent humidity and 82 degrees.

Meanwhile, his theatrical career, which was supposed to go into eclipse in his retirement, has blossomed. He has the starring role in *Riven* (to be released October 1997), the sequel to the best-selling CD-ROM computer game, *Myst*, and is in demand at athletic events to offer his rousing unaccompanied rendition of "The Star-Spangled Banner," which he does in a still-resonant tenor voice.

He is frequently invited to compete in marathons in foreign cities, offers which he finds difficult to turn down. John is busier in retirement than he was when he worked full-time, which is just fine by him.

Back in the late 1960s and early 1970s a bit of confusion developed over the fact that there were a number of road racers who turned in very notable performances but who never seemed to do any speedwork. They never went to the track and in fact, in some cases, avoided the track like the plague. They ran high mileage during their typical week, but appeared to do no speedwork, yet their performance was outstanding.

What observers of this phenomenon failed to consider, probably because it was staring them right in the face, was that these runners raced virtually every weekend, everything from 5K to 20 miles and beyond. So although they did no speedwork during the week, their racing every weekend provided their speedwork under the guise of racing.

If you've never done any road racing but you do want to improve your performances, it is best to ease into the racing scene. Start with relatively short races, like the very popular 5K, and don't jump into a racing routine where you immediately begin racing every weekend. Race once a month at first. Make certain to keep in mind the age-old rule of racing: the longer the race, the shorter the warm-up; the shorter the race, the longer the warm-up.

If you are going to race a 5K, jog a mile easily to warm up, then do a half-dozen easy sprints to stretch your legs. Go out at a speed which you have determined in advance is within the realm of possibilities based upon your weekday workouts. To speed through the first mile two or three minutes under your average weekday workout pace is soaked with glory, but it is embarrassing to come doddering across the finish line at a pace two or three minutes slower than your weekday pace.

When you line up at the start, line up in the field at a spot that appears to be comparable with the pace you plan to run. Don't line up in the front unless you plan to win the race outright. To line up in front impedes faster runners and can cause accidents as faster runners are forced to work their way around you.

If you run a race realistically based upon your current capabilities, you'll be able to increase your pace as you come within sight of the finish line and will probably pass masses of runners who weren't as judicious as you were with their pace. Judiciousness is something older runners have in abundance.

Racing is a worthy challenge and highlight to your weekday workouts, it can put a real edge on your running generally, it is a nice social opportunity to be with others who share your interest in running, and it is a very effective way to sneak that speed workout in without hardly noticing it.

If you haven't joined a running club, consider doing so. Besides the social aspects, running clubs often organize buses or car pools to go to races you might not otherwise consider. For information on races for 50+ running, subscribe to *National Masters News* ($26/year) at P.O. Box 16597, North Hollywood, CA 91615-9881.

Resting

People who run are not typically people with a lot of spare time on their hands. People who run are typically busy people who fit their running in around full lives or who fit part of their full lives in around their running. The tendency of runners to be "doers" rather than "watchers" is both one of their greatest strengths and a potential weakness that could undermine running to their potential.

There are four basic elements of training: endurance, strength, speed, and rest. Most runners do well when it comes to building an endurance base. Some also do well incorporating strength and speed. But few runners take the rest part of the equation seriously. Yet there is evidence in abundance that of the four basic elements, rest is the most important. Tom Osler, a pioneer of longer-distance running, put it this way in his classic 1978 book, *Serious Runner's Handbook:* "Rest is as important as stress when building a runner's base."

Some world-class marathoners learned the importance of rest by accident. Twice in the late 1960s, Australian Derek Clayton was hobbled with injuries to the point where he needed to undergo surgical operations to correct lower leg problems. In both instances, he came off the forced rest to set

world records in the marathon, one of them (2:08:34 in Antwerp on May 30, 1969) which stood for more than a dozen years. A similar situation involved Joan Benoit. Hobbled with Achilles tendon and knee problems, she underwent surgery that forced her to stop running. She went on from this forced rest to win the first women's Olympic marathon in 1984.

An ongoing running program offers a rainbow of benefits, but every benefit we enjoy in life comes at a price. In the case of running, the price is a constant cycle of tearing down and rebuilding muscle and tissue. Hopefully, the rebuilding brings the muscle back stronger than it was before it was rested.

But within the rebuilding process, the recuperation of muscle and tissue needs an environment in which it can occur uninterrupted. Never more so than with mature runners. A muscle cannot constantly be tested and retested without ultimately breaking down. In running, we refer to the breaking down as "overuse." In essence, "overuse" is simply using and reusing something until it breaks.

Oil Those Hinges

Think of a garden gate. If it is not used, the hinges rust, and when they are finally used again, they often snap. If the gate is used regularly and properly maintained, it works smoothly and effortlessly. But if it is overused, it wears out and malfunctions. There is nothing especially complicated about this process. Work a series of muscles, give them time to recuperate, and they bounce back stronger.

In the older runner, the same basic theory applies, but with one difference: work a series of muscles, then give those muscles *additional* time to recuperate. As we age, the capacity of our muscles to do work diminishes, but only gradually. Which is why some 60-year-old runners regularly beat runners half their age. And why, as we discussed several chapters ago, 90-year-old sedentary people who seemed primed for the physical trash heap can be turned around by taking up a muscle-strengthening routine. As we age, what changes most is our recuperative powers. We can still do nearly the same work we did 20 years ago, but it takes us longer to recuperate.

This is a simple fact of life, not something that is optional. We can't say, "Well, this may apply to others, but it certainly doesn't apply to me!" It applies to all of us. And a failure to recognize the fact that we need more recuperation time leads to one eventuality: overuse injury. Which is one of the reasons older runners tend to suffer injuries more than their younger counterparts. The older runners' heads still think they are 20 years younger, while their bodies know they aren't.

So what are we to do? Just bag our running because we're older and need more recuperation time? No. What we need to do is merely moderate our training program and our racing frequency so that we allow the body the time it needs to come back strongly from hard workouts and tough races.

Certainly, due to genetic factors, not every body is created equal. Some runners need more recuperation time than others based on the same workouts. But certain commonalities come along with aging, and one is this general tendency to need more time to recuperate.

Rules of the Road

Certain rest-oriented rules can be applied to our running in order to keep us healthier, uninjured, and running better:

• *Run fewer days a week.* There are some runners who glory in having run every day for the last 30 years, even if some of those runs were hobbling around a parking lot on crutches. If you've been running six to seven days a week, consider five to six or even four to five days (with some substitute, low-impact workouts).

• *Substitute low-impact workouts for running on one or two days a week.* Aerobic, sweat-breaking workouts on stairclimbing machines, exercise bicycles, or in a pool provide good aerobic capacity without beating up your legs. All three of the above mentioned are also excellent for building the strength in the quads, something only hill running does to the same extent.

• *Work some walking into your running workouts, either before, during, or after—or all three* (see chapter 8).

• *Race less to race better.* If you are used to racing every weekend at a variety of distances, cut back. Racing, although exhilarating, is also wearing. Apply the formula of giving yourself one day away from racing for every mile you race. If you have been used to racing three times a month, cut back to two. Besides giving your body time to recuperate from hard workouts, you may actually find your racing performances enhanced. If you are a marathoner over 50, consider doing no more than two marathons a year. Recuperating from a marathon is a lengthy process and it is only the genetically endowed

50+ runner who can recuperate sufficiently to do well in more than two marathons a year.

• *Establish and stick to "down" periods during the year when you cut back to maintenance running and do not race.* This is easy enough to do in areas where the seasons of the year are extreme. But in areas with mild temperatures year-round, it may take a special force of will to adhere to backing your running down over the winter in order to allow your muscles and tissues to heal before adding strength and speed workouts come spring. The long-range benefits, if your plan is to run the rest of your life, are worth the discipline needed to rest creatively.

• *Regularly schedule deep-tissue massage.* The older we get, the more help we can use in bringing our muscles and tissues back. Unfortunately, if we've been running for years upon years, we've managed to build up a fair amount of microscopic (and some not-so-microscopic) scar tissue. A regular session of deep-tissue massage therapy with a qualified sports massage specialist will do wonders toward improving your running, turbocharging your recuperation from training and racing, and extending the useful life of your body. By "regular session" I don't mean daily, although for the hard-core athlete, a daily massage would work wonders. "Regular" can be once every two weeks or even once a month. But it should be "regular," it should be deep tissue, and it should be administered by someone who is trained in applying the correct pressure at the correct angle to the affected muscles and tissues. Many a world-class runner could have extended his or her career by getting the knots out. You're never too old to start the process.

• *Apply the same theories to your personal life.* Just as our lives away from running can be affected (either positively or negatively) by how our running is going, our running can be affected by how the rest of our life is going at the time. Many of us tend to want to do more, more, more. And certainly, for those so inclined, modern life offers any variety of activities for the ambitious. But there are some people who follow the theory that nature abhors a vacuum. These folks think that if there is an empty box on their calendar, its existence is a sin against nature, and they take great pains to fill the box with something, anything so that it is not blank. Faced with a blank calendar box, these folks begin to decompensate. They become nervous, irritable, frantic. We need to learn to rest and relax as well as we've learned to go, go, go. Resting and relaxing is an art—but an art well worth pursuing. By learning to rest and relax creatively, you'll teach your body—and your mind—to come back stronger.

chapter

7

Pacing

*"All great achievements
require time."*

—David Joseph Schwartz

Most of us, when we were kids, knew someone who died tragically while in high school. It was usually in a car wreck. A Deadman's Curve kind of thing. A life tragically and forever cut short in the flower of youth and all that. A kid who, because his life stopped at 17, will always remain 17 in our memories, while the rest of us gradually age our way from one reunion to the next.

We tend to romanticize these people for the lives unled, assuming for them great things, marvelous accomplishments, the potential to excel, when in reality they would probably today still be pumping gas at Grummand's Exxon.

The Benefits of Effective Pacing

In reality, we would do better to reward with our romantic notions those who paced their lives so well that they're still going. Such as the hero of a 1996 summer biathlon. No, not the run/bike/run variety of biathlon. This is the traditional biathlon that comes to us by way of the Winter Olympics, where athletes cross-country ski and pause at various stations along the way

to shoot at targets. The summer biathlon is this: run a mile, shoot five shots at a target from a prone position, run a mile, shoot five shots from a standing position, then run another mile. For each target hit from a prone position, 15 seconds are subtracted from the total time; for each target hit from the standing position, 30 seconds are subtracted.

The hero of the day wasn't the overall winner but a man 79 years old who was back for his third year at this particular biathlon, who chugged patiently but inexorably along the very hilly mile course, doing each mile within 10 seconds of the others, and who shot tolerably well. This man was the personification of reasonable pacing. He was also well pleased with himself that day, and deserved to be: he'd bettered his 1995 time by nearly 90 seconds. Asked for the secret of his success when he went up to receive his award: "Start at a pace you know you can keep until the finish."

We are led to believe that as we mature, our sense of pacing increases, that we automatically become wiser in the ways of the world. To some extent, and for some people, this is true. We experience enough instances of bad pacing when we are young that the realization eventually sinks in that there is something to be said for spreading our limited energies out over the long run instead of sprinting them away in the first mile.

Yet there are quite a few mature runners who consistently undermine their own performances by ignoring the importance of pacing. Go out too fast on a workout or a race and you pay the price with a strained and painful second half, a situation that is not conducive to eagerly anticipating your next workout or race.

This shortcoming is usually due to one of two causes:

- The runner never learned pacing in spite of living more than 50 years.
- The runner is attempting to run at the same speeds he or she did 10 years ago.

In both instances, the results are the same: frustration.

On any given day, each of us who runs is capable of covering a specified distance in a specific time—or in a slower time. But never in a faster time. We cannot humanly achieve this ideal time every day. We approach that ideal time for the specified distance when we race. When we train, we typically do so at a time slower than we are capable. This builds upon our endurance and enhances the training effect.

But whether it is in training or racing, if we go out at a pace faster than we are capable of maintaining over the entire distance, we begin to slow down. The faster we go out beyond our capabilities, the quicker we will slow down because we rapidly outrun ourselves and our current abilities.

Some runners do this consistently. It's just how they've been taught or how they've taught themselves to run. They do everything full tilt. They are typically not longer-distance runners because they are physically incapable of running very far at that speed. Or if they do run longer distances, their longer workouts and races are miserable messes throughout the second half.

It is not the height of genius to conclude that the ideal and simplest pacing is even pacing. If you are going to do a five-mile workout at 70 percent effort and a 9:00 pace would accomplish that, stay steady at the 9:00 pace for the entire five miles. Such pacing keeps life simple, and it produces predictable results.

Rhythmic Pacing

There has been a great deal of discussion over the decades concerning pacing. And all the discussions of effort-adjusted pacing, or of negative (second) split pacing, merely muddies the waters.

Arthur Lydiard, the world's foremost distance coach, lists proper pacing among the 11 essential factors needed for a runner to reach racing potential. Way back in the 1970s, *Runner's World* editor Joe Henderson put it this way: "Generally, it's pace that kills, not distance."

"I'm pretty sure one's best times in races are achieved as a result of even pacing," Bill Rodgers said. "If I've had any success in racing, this is one of the major reasons why. In my training and in my racing, I've tried to run at a steady, rhythmic pace."

"A factor in marathon racing that is of supreme importance is the even pace," said Manfred Steffny, editor of the German running magazine *Spiridon*. "In no other sport will you gain so much from an ability to apportion your energy carefully. Poor pacing is disastrous; usually it takes the form of going out too fast."

The 1973 Boston Marathon winner, Jon Anderson, put it this way: "If one is to race effectively, he must realize what pace to begin the race at—this is the key to being able to finish the race effectively."

Although it is the simplest form of pacing, even pacing isn't simple, due in large part to the human physiology. For instance, on any given training run that lasts more than 30 minutes, the first several miles are stiff and sluggish because the muscles are cold and the cardiovascular system is going through various gears in an effort to get up to speed. If you are capable of running a 7:00 mile but are training today at a 9:00, your first two miles at 9:00 will involve some effort. However, once the big muscles in your legs warm and your cardiovascular system clicks into overdrive, 9:00 miles begin to come easy. Almost too easy. The tendency is to pick up the pace because now 9:00s seem like a strain because they are way too slow and inefficient for the place your body is physically.

If, however, you have set yourself the goal of doing this workout at a 9:00 pace, you need to practice discipline to hold yourself back, and for some people, that's close to impossible. Many people, especially those who train but do not race, run like they feel. If they feel good, they pick up the pace. If they feel like the current pace is too much work, they drop it back. This is all well and good if there is no specific goal in mind. The problem with running on a regular basis but with no goals in mind is that the running tends to become hollow and dispirited.

Further, the problem with translating a "run as you feel" philosophy to your racing is that it, too, causes frustration because performance is consistently undermined by bad pacing. There's nothing more discouraging than struggling in over the second half of a race while being passed by half the field. Better to start slower and be the passer in the latter stages than the passee.

And that can only be done by good pacing, which in turn can be accomplished by good and realistic planning before ever lining up to race, and by regularly running accurately-measured courses or regularly running at the track in training so you can establish a sense of pace.

The Ironic Dichotomy

There is a fascinating ironic dichotomy present in running: many people who become involved in distance running come from a very structured background and approach their running as a safety valve from that strictly controlled life, resisting anything (like a track or a 16-week training schedule) that places boundaries on their running. Oddly enough, there are millions of runners who come from the same background who love how easy it is to translate the same familiar, nearly scientific structures to running.

Which is one of the ways that a pursuit as simple as running is actually so complex: how can people of the same mind-set *expect* to get—and actually *get*—such different results from the same activity? On one hand, an escape from the structured life; on the other, an inner peace created by the structure they can bring to it.

This is not to say there is no benefit to the unstructured running program. Run like you feel if it makes you feel better. But don't expect predictable results.

Way back there where we discussed the two reasons for facing frustration, the second involved training at pacing levels that were reasonable 10 years ago but that have not been modified to realistically accommodate your abilities today. This is not to say that we should not set ambitious goals for ourselves. But we will only frustrate ourselves (and in the process shorten our useful running life) if we don't leaven our ambitious goals with the reality of where we are at physically. Our muscle strength and speed is not the same at 55 as it was at 33. Which is why races are broken into age-group competitions and why there are age-adjusted performance charts available.

The fastest way to burn out is to constantly shoot for—and fall far short of—unrealistic goals. We need to shift our sights from dwelling on glories of the past to setting our sights on realistic and attainable glories for the future. And the only way to reach those goals is to train and race at a pace that inches us closer to them instead of frustrating us by rushing us forward.

If it involves a weekly non-gut-wrenching session at the track where a pace is easily measured and where there are no interruptions by traffic blocking an intersection up ahead, it is almost always worth the effort.

It is worth stealing one of Elaine LaLanne's favorite aphorisms: "Make haste slowly."

One of the most remarkable marathon performances on American soil came at Boston in 1975. Bill Rodgers, then in his 20s, had tried the marathon distance before and failed, but was coming off a very successful world cross-country championship race. He ran Boston wearing a motley T-shirt with the letters *GBTC* (Greater Boston Track Club) crudely drawn on the front. He appeared to be unusually relaxed. Instead of sprinting through aid stations, he walked through them, drinking his fill of water, before rolling back into his characteristic light-footed stride. At one point in the late miles of the race, he even stopped to kneel down in the middle of the road to tie his shoe. He crossed the finish line in 2:09:55, the first time an American had broken 2:10.

Today there is a seemingly revolutionary movement among running experts who preach scheduling walking breaks into your training and racing as a way of extending the range of your runs, mitigating the negative effects of working the same muscles over and over and over, hastening recovery from long runs and from races, and even improving performance in longer events.

The two principal proponents today of using walking breaks are Jeff Galloway, 1972 Olympic 10,000-meter runner, and Joe Henderson, West Coast editor of *Runner's World* and one-time (1970–77) editor of that magazine.

Both acknowledge that the concept is nothing new. In the 1960s, the practice of walking within your running program was preached by New Jerseyite Tom Osler, a pioneer in ultrarunning. In the previous century, "pedestrianism" was much more popular than running, and produced some performances during six-day races that have only been matched within the last decade. We're talking pedestrians who regularly covered more than 500 miles in six days!

Today's "semi-pedestrianism" is preached by Jeff Galloway and Joe Henderson for all the right reasons, especially reasons that should interest a 50+ runner: injury prevention, increase of longest workout, graduation to ultra events, quicker (and more thorough) recovery, easier access to the marathon.

Naturally, the two prophets have their detractors—hardcore runners who feel that to walk is to admit defeat, that to walk makes you a walker and not a runner, that to use walking within your runs is, well, wimpy.

Weighty Arguments for Walking

It is easy for us to understand the purists' stand. But Galloway and Henderson bring a lot of weight to their stand in that both of them were among the hardest core of hard-cores when it came to running, and both have seen the wisdom Tom Osler preached decades ago.

Tom Osler, a retired mathematics professor at Glassboro State College in New Jersey, won three national championships (25K, 30K, and 50 miles) in the mid-'60s. In 1978 Osler wrote his second book, *Serious Runner's Handbook*, a volume that quickly became a classic. The book was constructed as a series of 255 questions with Osler's answers. Here is Question #31:

Can I use walking mixed with running rather than a continuous run?

A: Yes, if continuous running seems too hard. A runner in fairly good condition might want to run continuously at a steady speed and reserve walking mixed with running for those days when he feels a bit bushed. For the novice, walking might be necessary in most workouts.

I find it convenient to walk briskly for five minutes following every 20 minutes of running. More walking seems to leave my legs heavy and unwilling to run again. Be sure to walk with vigor, as it is necessary to keep the circulation moving. Don't stroll as you would at a shopping mall. A slow walk does the legs harm, as the blood is not forced back to the heart through the capillaries. For me, walking at about 3.5 miles per hour is appropriate, but this is an individual matter.

For the 50+ runner, walking can be the secret ingredient that keeps the running program on track and healthy. It is a good practice to use walking as bookends to the daily run.

A quarter-mile walk as a warm-up before running will loosen stiff muscles and will massage them through a range of motion different from the running process. A quarter-mile of walking at the end of a workout for each four to five miles run will serve as a cool-down while also helping prevent the pooling of blood below the waist, a condition that can cause excessive strain on the heart. Dr. Kenneth Cooper believes this condition may have been a contributing factor in the death of Jim Fixx.

Walking scheduled into running workouts or races can serve to lower the working heart rate, extend a runner's potential range, and speed recovery. But when using walking within a running program, the walking must be used from the start if it is to be effective. Anyone can walk in the latter stages of a workout or race, and many runners do—but not because it was part of their plan, but rather because they outran their training level in the early going and simply ran out of steam.

Keep the Walking Program Simple

There is a variety of ways to work walking into a run. But like everything else in life, the simpler you can keep it, the better. The walking can be simply a one-minute brisk walk at the end of every mile. Or it can be a 1-minute walk every 8 minutes or 9 minutes or 10 minutes. The best way of

scheduling in the walking is to avoid complicated math because in the latter stages of a long race, a runner's brain doesn't do math well.

Jeff Galloway, a 50+ runner and a very fast one at that, is very persuasive in his admonitions to use walking inside your running. His contention is that each walking break massages the leg muscles by breaking them out of the repetitive running motion and into a different series of motions. When the minute is done, gently roll into the running motion. By incorporating this process from the start of a long run or race, you may find yourself unusually fresh near the end and able to drop the last four or five walking breaks entirely. In the process you might pick up your per-mile pace, while if you'd run the whole way, the tendency at that point would be to begin slowing.

In a long race, it is advisable to walk through the aid stations, both as a convenient way of incorporating a walking break and as a way of making it as easy as possible to drink as much fluid as you want. Most of us are not talented enough to continue running while drinking; more of the fluid gets on us than in us.

For runners who race at 7:00-per-mile or faster, Jeff advises a 15-second shuffle pace through aid stations and as a regular "rest" every 10 minutes or so. The shuffling serves to massage the legs and also brings down the working heart rate. The time lost in walking for a minute or shuffling for 15 seconds is minimal because you are still moving forward.

An additional benefit of working walking into your workouts and races is that the change in biomechanics during the walking phase gentles down the effort and begins the recovery process while you are still exercising. The recovery process can be further moved along by the practice of walking a quarter-mile at the end of the workout or race for each four to five miles run.

Some older runners are also finding it valuable to schedule in brisk walking days once or twice a week instead of regular runs. The walking helps them recover while they are still exercising, helps pump built-up waste products out of their legs, and prevents injuries by essentially giving the legs days off while they are still working to keep the fitness level up.

Access to the Marathon

There are literally dozens of marathon-training clinics around the U.S. and in Canada that are built on Jeff Galloway's theories of working walking in with your running. And the success rate of these neophyte marathoners is astonishing. It's well over 95 percent.

As you might imagine, when a runner moves up to the challenging and esoteric world of ultrarunning, walking becomes even more important. Tim Twietmeyer, four-time winner of the Western States 100 Trail Run, the granddaddy of all 100-milers, walks roughly 15 percent of the course. Based on 100 miles, that's extremely easy math: Tim walks 15 miles—and still wins the race.

The late Dick Collins, a 60+ locomotive of a runner who ran literally hundreds of marathons and ultras, carefully scheduled walking breaks. Dick was sometimes known as the Paper Cup Man. When Dick went to a track to run/walk a 24-, 48-, 72-hour, or six-day race, he placed a paper cup just off the running surface of the track at the beginning and end of both straightaways. Then, for days on end, he circled the track, running the straightaways and walking the curves, the paper cups doing all of his thinking for him, like signals along a railroad line.

John Keston, age-group world-record holder at nearly a dozen distances (3:00:58 marathon at age 71) does walking workouts two days a week and walks a portion of each of the first 20 miles in a marathon. He uses a heart rate monitor and claims the walking breaks bring down his heart rate significantly, allowing him more energy to expend in the latter miles of a race.

Although the occasional 50+ runner prefers to stick to the strict "run every step or you aren't a runner" philosophy, an increasing number of older runners are learning new tricks, and walking before you need to in order to run better later in the race is one trick that goes a long way.

III

The Art and Science of Ingestion

chapter

9

Hydrating

*"The last and often forgotten
nutrient for healthy
aging is water."*

—Sharon Bortz, MS, RD

We are often told that whether we see the glass half full or half empty indicates our outlook on life: positive or negative, respectively. Actually, our perception of where the water stands in the glass may merely be a response to our current state of hydration.

There is no single dietary element in a runner's existence nearly as important as that element that has no calories, no dietary nutrients, no nothing beyond itself—water. Yet Ellen Coleman, an exercise physiologist, registered dietitian, and veteran of the Hawaii Ironman Triathlon, says, "Water is the most essential of all nutrients, since your body requires it constantly."

Before there were sport drinks, there was water. Before there was life on Earth, there was water. Plants and animals consist primarily of water. Without water, there is no life. Yet too few of us drink nearly enough water to sustain our body's needs.

Never Underestimate the Importance of Water

The role of water is even more important to the mature individual—and especially to the mature exercising individual. We've all heard the admonition that we should drink eight glasses of water a day. And it's true: we should each drink *at least* eight glasses of water a day. If we're exercising regularly, we should drink considerably more than that.

There are five benefits that sufficient ingestion of water bestows on the mature person:

• *It promotes adequate blood volume and viscosity,* which in turn promotes more efficient transportation of oxygen and nutrients to the far reaches of the body while more effectively removing waste and damaged cells. Sufficient blood volume and viscosity also make life easier on the heart because it is much easier for the heart (the body's pump) to move blood that is free-flowing than it is to move blood that is thick and sludgy. We need to think of the blood vessels in our bodies as rivers of commerce. Just like the Mississippi and its tributaries, a great deal of vital freight is moved up and down the river on barges and on passenger vessels. Think of the barges as carrying nutrients up the river of our blood supply, think of the passenger-filled riverboats as an oxygen supply; then, on the other hand, think of the garbage scows coming down the river as damaged cells and waste matter being carried from the remote parts of our bodies by the intricate system of capillaries and vessels, to ultimately be excreted. Now, what happens to our crowded, busy river of commerce if there is a drought, if the supply of water on which all this commerce floats is cut back? Barges go aground, river traffic slows and stalls. It isn't much different within our bodies. Our daily ingestion of water is emptied from the stomach into our internal river. Much of the water is used in our blood, some is taken from the bloodstream to bathe our cells so they can work more efficiently. Some is shunted off to our skin where it is used to cool us by carrying heat away from the skin in the form of sweat. If the available water is insufficient, especially insufficient to provide for the exercising body, our efficiency is severely compromised.

• Sufficient ingestion of water *significantly aids regularity,* a growing concern for people (especially women) as they age. We used to always joke about how older people seemed to spend so much time discussing their bodily functions. The concern with bodily functions, especially with regularity, is extremely important. Regularity is vital to good health. Fecal matter that remains in the body for extended periods of time drains the body of energy and becomes increasingly dangerous from a bacterial standpoint.

• The *normal functioning of joints and internal organs* is dependent on a ready supply of water. Deprive the body of water, and the lubricating fluids in the joints are compromised beyond what they are by the natural process of aging. Also, virtually every organ in the body is dependent upon water for its smooth function; cut back on water intake, and the regular function of virtually every organ, from the pancreas to the kidneys (and including the brain) is compromised.

• *Healthy skin* is dependent on an adequate supply of water. You can use all the moisturizers you want on the outside of the skin, but if the cells that comprise the skin are not properly bathed in water, the skin is going to dry out and many of its functions will be inhibited. Think of your skin as thousands upon thousands of interconnected lakes. When filled, they are smooth-functioning and healthy. Bring on a drought and they dry out and everything about them dies. As we age, and especially as we age and continue to run in the natural world, which can tend to prematurely age skin, the ideal situation is to shelter the surface of the skin with sunblock and moisturizer and at the same time keep the skin supple from the inside out with adequate water intake.

• Healthy skin and sufficient water *promote natural cooling of the body by sweating.* Sweating is good for the skin because it exercises the skin and cleanses it of impurities that build up by expelling those impurities. The process of cell and pore cleansing is especially important as we age if we are to maintain healthy skin. Sweating is also good because it is the human being's very effective way of regulating core temperature so it stays within ideal parameters. Exercising, of course, raises the body's core temperature and teaches the body to perspire more efficiently. Fluids lost by sweating must be replaced by the ingestion of additional water to keep the exercising body bathed in fluid and to maintain a fluid balance.

Ellen Coleman calls water "the most commonly overlooked endurance aid." In her book *Eating For Endurance*, Coleman advises runners to drink three to six ounces of fluid every 10–15 minutes "to replace sweat losses and maintain blood volume." Annette Cain, who has a degree in nutrition science from the University of California at Davis, adds an additional benefit: water decreases fluid retention. "Water retention from hormones and excess salt can be eliminated by drinking more water," she says. This is a concept for older runners to grasp and use, since most of us have—mistakenly—been led to believe that drinking water causes water retention, when in reality it flushes out excess fluid.

Water and the Exercising Body

The human body is a marvelous machine that, unlike machines of metal and plastic, improves its function the more it is used. While a lawnmower or a car wears itself out the more it is used, the human body works just the opposite. If you don't use it regularly for what it was designed, it begins to fall apart. On the other hand, if you make regular use of it, it improves its function.

If you judiciously run more and more, your body learns in the process to run better. If we could translate that same phenomenon to the automotive world, except for those instances where we crash our car beyond repair, we should each need to purchase only one car in a lifetime, and the more regularly we used it, the newer it would become—while maintaining its classic lines.

That is literally what happens when we run through the various age stages of our life: we become physically better than expected while maintaining certain classic lines. And the entire process is fueled by water. The process could not, in effect, happen without water—and lots of water.

The most important process water facilitates in running is sweating. The process of perspiring within the human being is a complex cascade of chemical reactions unavailable to other animals. It is a fact that a well-trained human being can run down any animal on Earth by wearing that animal down. The animal is worn down by its inability to efficiently disperse into the surrounding atmosphere heat that is created by its exercising body. As a result, the animal overheats and collapses, while the much more efficiently cooling human being just keeps coming and coming and coming.

Atmospheric conditions, of course, dictate how difficult or easy it will be to cool the exercising body. If the atmosphere is dry, the body cools more easily because the perspiration evaporates almost immediately upon surfacing from the skin, thereby very efficiently dispersing the body's heat into the surrounding atmosphere. On the other hand, if it is humid, cooling the body becomes a much more difficult task because the perspiration, when it comes to the surface of the skin, is not immediately evaporated and besides bathing the skin in heat-laden sweat, it impedes any subsequent perspiration from dispersing heat brought to the surface.

When we run regularly, over a period of time our body learns to become more effective in perspiring in two ways:

- Whereas a novice runner will exercise for several miles before "breaking a sweat," the veteran runner's body breaks a sweat very early on, having learned over years that the initiation of exercise usually signals a prolonged session of exercise. The body, in effect, learns to get a jump on the cooling process.

- The other thing that happens is that the experienced runner's perspiration is not the same as that of a novice runner. This difference is primarily seen in the large amounts of salt that the inexperienced runner's body excretes through perspiration, while the experienced runner's body perspires a much more salt-free fluid, jealously holding onto salt that may be needed later.

Several of us who in 1989 were training to become the first runners to go from Badwater in Death Valley to the peak of Mt. Whitney and back in the middle of summer (a distance of 300 miles) spent extended periods of time training and living in the desert. We were periodically joined by running friends who did occasional workouts with us. In the wake of one lengthy discussion on the exercising body's ability to retain salt when trained to do so, we took turns licking each others' arms at the end of a four-hour workout to see which of us were more desert trained. Naturally, those of us who had been training regularly in the heat were nearly salt-free while those who had just the day before come down to join us were nearly as salty as some of the nearby salt flats. This ability to retain salt comes in handy for older runners who are concerned about high blood pressure; if you can train your body to retain salt, salt that the body needs to function well, there is no need to ingest additional salt that can contribute to increasing blood pressure.

The Art of Emptying

The discussion of efficient sweating needs to be joined by a discussion of what occurs several steps back of the process of cooling by sweat: how does the water get from the glass or water bottle to the surface of the skin by way of the stomach?

When considering the subject of fluid processing from the stomach to where it is needed, there are two points that are extremely important to keep in mind:

- From the time you pour fluid into your stomach, it takes a minimum of 45 minutes for that fluid to be absorbed and shunted out to various other parts of the body where it can be useful. Fluid that is colder is absorbed faster by the stomach.

- Just because you pour fluid into the stomach does not mean that it automatically goes to where it is needed.

For the runner (especially for the long-distance runner), the implications of these two facts are enormous. Obviously, if you are running a marathon and have a half-hour left to run, taking fluid at the next aid station isn't going to be any help getting you across the finish line—although it will begin to help you rehydrate, and therefore to recuperate, following your marathon.

Since it takes a minimum of 45 minutes for fluid to empty from the stomach and do some good, it is obvious that a runner should be drinking well in advance of needing the fluid. The old saying is that if you're thirsty during a race, you're in trouble. The reasoning is obvious: if you're thirsty and it takes 45 minutes minimum for the stomach to process fluid, for the next 45 minutes of running, you're going to be doing it in fluid deficit, which means that the body is going to be working against itself, straining unnecessarily. The older the runner, the more he or she needs every advantage when striving to exercise regularly and well. Good hydration is an excellent starting point for allowing well-used, mature body organs to function well and longer. Remember also that adequate water intake helps prevent urinary infection and kidney stone formation.

The best thing a runner can do is to remain constantly hydrated—even when not running. Sip water all day and your fluid reserves will remain filled, ready to be of assistance when you need them.

Which brings us to the second point: just because you dump fluid into your stomach does not mean it's going to do you any good. The stomach, like other body systems, must be taught what to do with the fluid it receives. People who do not regularly exercise when put into a hot environment or into forced exercise may drink plenty of fluid only to have it sit uselessly in their stomachs, where it causes bloating.

Even when fluid empties from the stomach, it doesn't necessarily go to where it is needed to cool the body and to help keep the blood volume up so that it can move nutrients through the bloodstream. Fluid that is emptied from the stomach can be absorbed by the body and end up between cells rather than inside the cells where it will be able to do some good; fluid trapped between cells (called intratissual or extra-cellular) gives the impression that your skin is bloated; getting the fluid out from between the cells and into the circulating blood volume or inside the cell walls can be a long process, certainly much too long to be of any value to the exercising body.

Once again, by sipping fluid (especially no-calorie water) all day, the body has plenty of non-stressful time to shunt the fluid to its parts that need it. Some people (again, older people) who are concerned about their weight, function under the misconception that by drinking water all day, they will put on weight because they will retain water. The facts are just the opposite. If the body is deprived of fluid, when it finally gets some it will tend to horde it, storing it wherever it can within the body. If, on the other hand, the body receives plenty of fluid each day (in fact, if it receives even an excess of fluid), it tends to excrete that which is not needed, effectively disposing waste products efficiently and without stress.

Which brings us to . . .

The Perfect Fluid Monitor

Fortunately, we are all equipped with a virtually perfect fluid level monitor. It is called the bladder. The extent of our ongoing hydration is properly measured by simple urine output. Of which there are two aspects:

- Volume
- Color

As properly-hydrated athletes, we should be urinating copiously six to eight times in each 24-hour period, and the urine should be as clear as water. Anything less indicates we're behind in our hydration and should step up the intake of water.

Sport Drinks: Do We Need 'Em?

In most instances, no, we don't. The ideal sport drink is water. Plain and simple. And the price is right.

Unless you are planning to exercise for hours upon hours, sport drinks are unnecessary and in many instances can adversely affect your workout. The problem with sport drinks is that they contain sugar (and it doesn't matter what form it comes in, it's still sugar) and once you begin ingesting sugar while exercising, you have to continue ingesting sugar or just as surely as you received a "lift" from it, you'll experience a drop without it.

It is also not advisable to drink sport drinks immediately before you exercise. The sugar in the sport drink instigates an insulin reaction, a process which diverts tremendous amounts of energy from what are about to be your working muscles. In reality, you've set your body up to be fighting against itself when you finally give it the go-ahead to exercise.

Sport drinks such as Gatorade and Exceed play a positive role if you are going to be exercising for more than two hours. Once you get out beyond two hours, your body can use nourishment along with its fluid intake. The sport drinks can provide that nourishment, although certainly a great deal of it comes in the form of simple sugar—but at that point, simple sugar is what your body craves. Again, though, the problem is that once you begin ingesting sugared sport drinks, you've got to keep taking in sugar or you'll crash.

DRINKING YOUR MEAL ON THE RUN

The prime fuel of the runner, and certainly the most easily processed, is liquid. Liquid is processed through the stomach with relatively little effort, thereby diverting a minimum of blood away from the working muscles.

Although it contains no nutrients, plain water is the most important liquid a runner can take—before, during, and after running. Water helps cool the exercising body, keeps the blood viscous enough to move nutrients around the body while removing damaged cells, and lubricates moving body parts.

For moderate running programs, water is essential and is literally all the runner needs beyond a well-balanced diet. However, when the runner moves up or out to longer distances in training and racing, there are distinct advantages to using carbohydrate-replacement drinks before, during, and/or after exercise.

Several decades ago, Gatorade was created as the replacement drink of choice, because it pretty much had the field to itself. Created to replace sweat lost during exercise, when it first hit the athletic market Gatorade literally tasted like sweat and was difficult to drink unless chilled to the extreme. Through a constant process of improving the product, Gatorade has been formulated in a number of flavors so that it is now tolerable in taste and fills the bill by replacing sugars and salts used up during extended exercise.

Based on Gatorade's success, numerous replacement fluids have come along, including Exceed and Performance. Most are very similar and are very good for the purpose of replacing essential fluids, sugars, and salts. A runner should be careful to dilute such drinks, however, as the manufacturers tend to mix them on the strong side. Mixed too strong, these drinks can upset the stomach. If you purchase the drinks in liquid form, cut them in half with plain water. If you purchase the drinks in powder form, mix them one-half to one-third of what the instructions call for.

It is difficult to go wrong in purchasing and using the basic athletic replacement fluids. Over the years, however, there has been a new crop of semi-athletic drinks that have sprung up that can be referred to as "liquid meals." Many of these are more identified with easily-digestible liquid nutrition for seniors, such as Ensure.

Back in the late 1970s, before there was a wide selection of athletic drinks for longer distance runners, some of us who ran 50-mile races used Nutrament liquid meals and Kerns fruit nectars for refueling during a race. They worked wonderfully and are again catching on among ultrarunners.

Within recent years, ultramarathoners have begun turning to the cornucopia of liquid meals for refueling during 50-mile, 100K, 100-mile, 24-hour, and multi-day races. The meals are relatively easy on the stomach, are processed faster by the stomach than solid foods, and provide a fair mix of carbohydrates, proteins, and fats. Unfortunately, all of that readily-available fuel comes at a price: the liquid meals are very high in calories.

Many seniors use liquid meals for part of their daily diet. Generally, that's not a good idea. Liquid meals are no substitute for a balanced diet of solid foods. This is especially important when we realize how important fiber is to a mature person's diet and regularity.

Use the following liquid meals to augment a regular diet during periods when you are running long on training runs or when you are racing long distances. It is not a bad idea to have a cold liquid meal ready as soon as you finish your long workout or race; the liquid meal is absorbed quickly and begins almost instantly to replace carbohydrates, proteins, and fats you've used up in your workout or race.

The following list is not complete; new brands are entering the market weekly. Calories are based on an eight-ounce serving, and carbs, protein, and fat are measured in grams. For simplicity's sake, we tested the drinks in vanilla flavor. Most taste like finely ground chalk with a vanilla disguise, but are delicious after a long workout if they are deeply chilled.

LIQUID MEALS FOR MATURE RUNNERS

Brand	Calories	Carbs	Protein	Fat
Boost	240	40	10	4
Endura Opt.	260	57	11	1
Ensure	250	40	9	6
GatorPro	360	58	16	7
Metabolol II	260	40	20	2
Nutrament	240	34	6.5	11
Nutra Start	210	40	10	2.5
Protein Repair	200	26	20	1.5
Sego Very	180	27	9	1
Sport Shake	310	45	11	10
Sustacal	240	33	15	6

Many ultrarunners who intend to be exercising more than two hours have experimented for years with getting their nutrition by eating solid foods, which tends to provide more real nourishment while putting something solid into the stomach. This may also have the effect of absorbing some of the stomach acids which can be produced during a long training run or race and which, if not diluted, can cause upset stomach.

Some ultrarunners never use sport drinks at all, but rely totally on solid foods (pretzels, baked potatoes, even turkey sandwiches) washed down with water. Ultrarunners are the athletic astronauts, and it has always been beneficial to monitor their experiments. Long before there was such a thing as Gatorade, ultrarunning pioneer Tom Osler was using heavily-sugared tea in his 24-hour track races.

Athletes who regularly do longer workouts and who want or need nourishment along the way have also been experimenting for years with drinks like Ensure and Nutriment with good results. Some ultrarunners have also found benefits in consuming carbonated mineral water after a long workout or race. The carbonation relieves gas trapped in the stomach and dilutes stomach acid, while the minerals help replace trace minerals used up in hard or long exercise.

Juices, Sodas, Beer

Fresh, canned, or bottled fruit juices can be used effectively in the latter stages of a long workout or in the wake of a workout. But once again, since there are natural sugars in the fruit juices, they should not be used in the early hours of a long workout. And once started during a workout, they need to be continued if you are to avoid crashing.

Except for the high-sugar high-caffeine colas that some runners favor in the latter stages of a race, soft drinks or carbonated drinks don't tend to be high on the list of liquids craved by runners. Frank Shorter has always favored defizzed cola in the later stages of a marathon. The double hit of caffeine and sugar can give a physiologically inspiring jolt.

Dave Welch, husband and coach of the world's best female masters marathon runner, Priscilla Welch, has a very sound philosophy toward nutrition for the athlete, and he's particularly down on carbonated drinks. "Too much phosphoric acid will destroy calcium in the muscle tissue," Welch claims.

At the other end of the "carbonated" scale, Dave Welch considers beer in moderation as the fifth food group. Beer and long-distance running seem to go together in some regions. Certainly, in moderation it contains a fair amount of carbohydrates and no fat. And there is the legend of Frank Shorter drinking two liters of German beer the night before he won the Olympic gold in Munich in 1972. On the down side, the alcohol in beer and wine does have a dehydrating effect on the athletic body, and can have a profound effect at the cellular level. Beer, in moderation, is best saved as a wind-down drink after a particularly satisfying workout.

In conclusion: drink water and lots of it on an ongoing basis. The well-hydrated body performs better and recovers faster.

Fueling

Jack LaLanne has been saying it for decades: if it comes down to a decision between a good diet or a good exercise program, you're better served by the latter. A body regularly engaged in a vigorous aerobic exercise program is like a furnace whose temperature is so intense that no matter what you throw into it to keep the fire going, it is devoured almost totally. On the other hand, a body that constantly sits around doing nothing physical can be fed the most scientifically precise beneficial diet and that body will not be truly healthy, because health is not merely the absence of disease, but the presence of fitness. The human body is designed to perform certain functions and most of those functions involve physical movement. Feed it perfect fuel (food) and if it does nothing with that fuel but merely exist sedentarily, what's the point?

The ideal body would be one that exercises regularly while being fueled with a quality array of fresh foods and avoids those foods that are detrimental (i.e., high fat and/or highly processed). The fresher the foods the better, especially when it comes to fruits and vegetables. Don't overlook the benefits of quick-frozen vegetables. These vegetables are usually more fresh than those found at produce counters, since the frozen vegetables are captured—and suspended—at their peak. Just don't lose all the nutrients by overcooking.

When it comes to food, people would have had to have been living in the bottom of a dark cave for the past 50 years to have no knowledge of which foods are good for them and which are bad. The atrocious diet of most Americans has nothing to do with lack of knowledge. Everyone in America knows that a McDonald's Big Mac is a dietary disaster while a fresh salad light on the dressing is a good source of vitamins, minerals, and roughage. Everyone knows a fresh Cinnabon is oozing with calories and fat while a plain bagel is fat-free and low in calories.

The most insidious sources of fats, sugars, and salts are highly processed foods: everything from canned soups to frozen burritos. The dietary value—or lack thereof—of any packaged food product in the U.S. is these days clearly defined on the label. There is no real excuse for eating badly. The dietary disaster in the U.S. is one of will—or rather, lack of will. Each of us needs to work up the will to eat well.

In many instances, however, when discussing this topic with runners over 50 years of age, it is like preaching to the converted. Although many 50+ runners willingly admit to having gone through stages of their lives when their diet was relatively atrocious (in the military or in college when they got by saving money subsisting on a diet of Coke and Kraft macaroni and cheese), most of them these days eat sensibly— much more sensibly than the average sitting-around sedentary American of the same age.

There are several reasons for this wisdom that comes with age, this sensible approach to eating:

• *Trial and error.* Sufficient years of experimenting have established that eating certain foods makes them feel alive while others turn them into slugs, something no runner wants to be.

• *Research.* The average 50+ runner is vitally interested in medical and dietary research. The average 50+ runner regularly reads reports on long-term studies involving exercise, diet, and fitness and takes the research to heart.

• *Performance.* The average 50+ runner already knows that with age, performances gradually diminish. But, with attention to areas such as proper recuperation from hard workouts and proper diet, that drop in performance can be minimized.

In talking with Amby Burfoot, the executive editor of *Runner's World* magazine and a 50+ runner, we learn that articles dealing with dietary secrets toward better running performances are among the most popular type of article the magazine carries. "Every runner is looking for an edge," Amby said at the 1996 Portland Marathon Race Directors' Workshop, "and apparently a lot of runners feel they can get that edge through dietary manipulation."

Amby, winner of the 1968 Boston Marathon, was for much of his running life a vegetarian, and very much an adept student of the fuel a runner consumes. Although no longer a strict vegetarian, Amby is very careful about his food intake, as are most of us.

Very Mixed Signals

"Dietary manipulation," a term that has negative connotations, best describes virtually every story we read on diet and nutrition today. And it is an apt term for what we, as mature runners, do with our diets.

"Manipulation" has negative connotations because it infers a person is "controlling" or is "using" a situation to his or her advantage. In discussing diet, especially diet for the performing athlete, the negative connotations inherent in "dietary manipulation" quickly switch. Of course we want to control and use our diet to our best advantage!

Do we want fad dieters to dictate to us what we eat? Do we care to be on the controlled end of someone else's "experiments" with nutrition? Not at our age. We've had plenty of opportunities over the years to make our own mistakes. We don't need someone else to make more mistakes for us. Which is why we can—and should—take nearly every article or report on diet with a (excuse the pun) grain of salt.

We read and hear incredible nutritional advice these days. It is almost as though if someone wants to make a boatload of money pitching a dietary manipulation program, the more bizarre it is, the more likely susceptible people will be to paying for it, while knowing subconsciously that it isn't really going to work.

We heard for years that fat is bad. Now we hear it is good. Especially for people who are exercising. Fat is good, carbohydrates are bad. Protein? Well, yeah, we need some of that for bigger muscles. The new grapefruit and soybean diet? Sounds new, hot, cutting edge. Better try it.

Unmixing the Signals

Let's get real. There are 10 basics of nutrition that apply to every human being over 50. We've all learned them by trial and error, and here they are:

• *If you eat more calories than you burn, you gain weight.* If you burn more calories than you eat, you lose weight. Nearly everything you put into your mouth contains calories (important exception: water). Calories that are not burned are converted by the body into fat and then stored. Consider this math: eat one Life Saver (about seven calories) per day over your caloric needs and by the end of the year you'll have added a pound of body weight; after 20 years, you're 20 pounds overweight—from just one little Life Saver per day.

• *Eat lots of fresh fruits and vegetables.* Fresh fruits and vegetables contain vitamins, minerals, and, frequently, fiber, which for the mature human body promotes regularity, a very good thing to promote.

• Less dense than fat and protein, *carbohydrates provide a good source of easily-digested fuel* for the working or exercising body. Most of your calories should come from carbohydrates. Dietitian Ellen Coleman recommends an athlete get 70 percent of the daily calories from carbohydrates, stressing fresh fruits, vegetables, and grains.

• *Protein is important for muscle development and maintenance.* Some protein in your diet is essential, especially if you are active. Pure protein tastes horrible, which is why it is often presented in conjunction with fat, which makes it palatable. But protein is also available in foods such as beans. Eat more beans.

• *Fat has received a bad rap* over the years not because it is inherently bad, but because most people eat too much of it. The body needs some fat in order to function properly. But we don't need anywhere the amount of fat present in the typical American diet. The problem with fat in the American diet is that it is hidden everywhere. Cut back on the fats, but don't cut them out. Don't ruin a perfectly nutritious salad by smothering it in fatty Thousand Island dressing; don't ruin a perfectly good bagel by covering it with fatty cream cheese.

• *Cut way back on your intake of the two white culprits: sugar and salt.* Virtually every processed food we eat is literally impregnated with sugar and salt. You don't need all that sugar and salt. Go out of your way to study labels in an attempt to avoid sugar and salt.

• *Avoid carbonated soft drinks of all kinds. Period.* You're paying a fortune and receiving nothing. Drink water instead. Or mix fruit juices with water to make them go farther; commercial juices are typically already too concentrated to start with.

• Whether or not you've ever done a marathon, *customize your ongoing diet* as though you were in the final week leading up to an important marathon. What works the week before a marathon works on a 52-week-per-year basis: heavy on carbs, drink plenty of fluids.

• *Don't eat late in the evening.* If you eat just before you go to bed, the calories are going to go straight into storage as body fat.

• *Eat slowly.* It takes roughly five minutes for your stomach to send the signal to your brain that you're full. You can stack on a load of excess calories in five minutes. Slow down. Enjoy your food. Savor your food. Stretch out the experience of eating. Pace yourself the way you do in a long workout or race when you eat.

The Question of Sportsbars

Sportsbars such as PowerBar have become so ubiquitous these days that you can find them everywhere, from the counter at Nevada casinos to the candy counter at movie theaters, in supermarkets, and in quickmarts at gasoline service stations.

Sportsbars were developed as a convenient way for an athlete to carry ready fuel on long workouts or races. Although some people use them as food, they are not meant to be a substitute for real food. A Pepsi and a PowerBar does not a balanced diet make, unless you're an astronaut. God forbid if that constitutes a "space age" meal. . . .

Because of their very nature, ounce-per-ounce sportsbars are an extremely expensive way to fulfill your basic nutritional needs for the day. You'd be much better off buying an apple, some fig bars, and a bagel, then washing all of it down with a big glass of water. Of course from a practical standpoint, on a long run a PowerBar is a lot easier—and a lot less messy—to carry than fig bars. If you've never used sportsbars on long workouts or during races, practice with them first. And always wash them down with plenty of water.

Common Sense Has No Calories

The bottom line on nutrition for the mature runner is very simple: Pause a moment before eating anything and objectively analyze what the end result will be of the food you're about to put into your mouth. Will it help your running? Will it maintain your good health? Will you be able to process it in a reasonable amount of time? And will it leave behind empty calories looking for a thigh on which to take up residence?

And keep in mind that as we age, we do not need the volume of food we did 30 or 40 years ago. Our youthful growth spurts, which required huge amounts of calories, are long behind us. Yes, our running stokes the metabolic furnaces within us, but we don't need to have mountains of food waiting for possible use as fuel during a potential lean period.

Eat to run; don't run to eat.

Pre-Fueling/
Re-Fueling

*"There's no such thing
as a bad carbohydrate."*

—Don Kardong

It is the rare runner who does not know the classic ritual of carbohydrate-loading. Carbohydrate-loading, once the preserve of the serious marathoner, has now become so ubiquitous that runners entered in a 5K race on Sunday spend Saturday evening carbo-loading. The fact that carbo-loading for a 5K will do little to enhance performance isn't the point. Carbo-loading has become a running ritual to the point that it has far outrun its original function. It has gone so far, in fact, that even people who don't run talk of carbo-loading, not unlike the term "world-class" being stolen from international athletic competition for use by the rest of the world.

Unfortunately, when anything becomes part of the landscape, its original serious function is diluted. So it is with carbohydrate-loading, although in this case, that is not all bad. The prevailing knowledge these days indicates that a mature runner would do well to apply a modified carbohydrate-loading to his or her diet on a daily basis. The feeling is that such a diet would benefit general physical health while also increasing running and racing performance.

To best understand this modern universal application of carbohydrate-loading to daily life, it is best to briefly review the evolution of carbohydrate-loading.

Carbo-Loading in Theory

It is not so many decades ago that the prevailing athletic knowledge indicated that prior to an athletic event, a great deal of food should be eaten to sustain the athlete through the coming contest. The typical "training meal" consisted of steak

and potatoes: protein and carbohydrates. But in a form that would "stick to your ribs" and that probably undermined many a potentially outstanding performance because so much blood had to be diverted to the stomach to process all that food that there wasn't much left to carry oxygen and nutrients to the working muscles.

As far as distance running went, research indicated that for efforts of an hour or more, the body's supply of fuel (glycogen) in the muscles and liver was very finite and would be quickly depleted. The secret was to increase the body's supply of glycogen by taking in and holding more carbohydrates.

A bizarre ritual was conceived by the Swedish physiologist Eric Hultman based on the theory that a sponge wrung dry would hold more water when next immersed. During the final week of training, the runner would do a last long, hard, "depletion" run that would use up as much stored glycogen as possible. The runner would then change over to a diet high in protein and fat and very low in carbohydrates. Of course, such a practice had two results: it broke the runner down physically and it made the runner a grouch. Neither event was especially positive during the final week leading up to a major race. During the final days before the race, the runner would change over to a carbohydrate-rich diet, the theory being that the body deprived of carbohydrates was now going to super-absorb all it could get, thereby filling and in fact topping off the fuel tanks.

Carbo-Loading in Reality

But even in the late 1970s, a few right-thinking scientists felt that the carbohydrate-loading with depletion phase was archaic. In his landmark book, *A Scientific Approach to Distance Running*, published in 1979, Dr. David Costill of Ball State University had this to say:

> *The keys to success in maximal glycogen loading are (1) to reduce the intensity and duration of your training runs to minimize the daily burn-off of both muscle and liver glycogen stores, and (2) to increase the percentage of carbohydrates in your diet. It may be*

true that training hard and abstaining from carbohy-
drates for several days before you start the carbohy-
drate loading procedure may stimulate a somewhat
higher glycogen storage, but I have my doubts. First,
the psychological trauma associated with carbohy-
drate starvation and hard training can unbalance the
psychological state of even the most dedicated
runners. More important, you should realize that
eating a high-carbohydrate diet and light training for
two or three days is sufficient to elevate your muscle
glycogen levels well above normal.

Subsequent research proved Dave Costill to be correct. Runners who ate a high-carbohydrate diet for three days before a marathon "soaked" up the same amount of glycogen as did those who suffered through the depletion phase. The major difference was that those who skipped the depletion phase skipped the suffering—and the potential physical and psychological breakdown that can open the runner to just about any stray germ or psychologically self-defeating notion that happens by. For the 50+ runner, this kinder, gentler carbo-loading is a godsend. As the body ages, it bounces back from stress more slowly. Why subject a well-trained, mature body to unnecessary depletion stress days before an important race or workout? The race or workout will provide plenty of stress on its own without going into it stressed out.

Carbo-Loading for You

The importance of a high-carbohydrate diet for the runner cannot be stressed enough. Even an average five-mile run depletes some of the runner's stores of glycogen, and they need to be replaced literally on a daily basis if the runner is to sustain any kind of training regimen. No fuel, no go.

Consequently, the most logical scenario is for the mature runner to customize the daily diet toward one very high in carbohydrates. For several days before an especially long run or race and for several days following such an effort, the proportion of carbohydrates in the diet should be further increased.

An increase in carbohydrates in the days following a long, hard effort is extremely important toward proper and sufficient recovery. And the recovery by the ingestion of carbohydrates should begin as soon after finishing the run as possible. If you carbo-loaded for three days before the race or run, carbo-reload for at least three days afterwards in order to restore the body to its full capacity.

When we think of carbo-loading we typically think of a huge plate of pasta. But carbohydrate-rich foods are everywhere. Rice is a good source of carbohydrates, as is bread, bagels, pancakes, fresh fruits, cereals (at least those low in sugar and salt, such as Cheerios and shredded wheat), oatmeal, and so on.

A bagel or a piece of toast or even pancakes eaten two hours before a long race or a long run give the stomach plenty of time to process the food through to the intestines, and provide some last-minute topping off of the fuel tanks. For many runners, they also provide an opportunity to absorb some of the stomach acid that typically forms due to the combination of an empty stomach and prerace nerves.

For especially long runs or ultramarathons, it is very beneficial to practice eating all sorts of solid carbohydrates, a little at a time, but on a regular and ongoing basis throughout your run, as a means of replacing burned carbohydrates and maintaining a settled stomach.

For the mature runner, a carbohydrate-rich diet is extremely beneficial because it is much easier on the stomach, is much more easily absorbed through the intestines, and is much more readily passed through the body in general.

As with any food, the body can better handle it and is less likely to convert it into fat and store it if the food is eaten in smaller portions three or four times a day instead of being eaten in one enormous gut-busting session. By spacing your more modest meals, you allow the body to more evenly meter energy, instead of pulling all available energy to the stomach for a marathon session of digestion.

It also goes without saying that most of us tend to eat much more than we need. It is always startling to see just how little East African runners eat when they visit industrialized nations to race. And of course they are some of the most talented longer distance runners in the world. The same can be said of the Tarahumara Indians of the Copper Canyon region of Mexico; they eat little more than corn and the occasional chicken, yet are able to cover incredible distances between sunrise and sunset.

We'd all do well to refrain from overtaxing our poor digestive systems on a daily basis.

chapter 12

Drugging

*"All I want to do is
drink beer and
train like an animal."*

**—Rod Dixon, sub-2:10
marathoner and sub-4:00 miler**

It has always been difficult for me to understand how, as a society, we can get across to children the seriousness of drug abuse when we have long referred to pharmacies as "drug stores." And further, as a society we've tended to glorify the wonders of drugs, consequently overprescribing them for every little ailment that comes along, while still touting the idea that "drugs are bad." On any given day in America, I don't think it would be far off the mark to say that there are many more people driving cars while under the influence of prescribed drugs such as Valium than there are under the influence of marijuana or alcohol.

The drugged-up problem becomes more pronounced the older the average American becomes. The medicine chest of the typical 65-year-old American looks like a 19th-century apothecary shop. As a society we tend to want to drug away the symptoms of diseases that, with a little work and forethought, we could have prevented in the first place. Why exercise to control high blood pressure when you can take a pill?

In some ways the legal drug culture has spilled over into running, where analgesics are consumed like M&Ms, a very dangerous trend, especially among older runners. In this chapter we'll examine analgesics, caffeine, alcohol, and endorphins as the four legal drugs and how they impact runners, running, and the mature athlete.

Analgesics: Running Candy

Many scientists believe that if aspirin had not been discovered some hundred years ago and instead was discovered today, its myriad properties would doom it to oblivion by the FDA because it is so potent in so many ways that it would never be approved as safe for use by human beings.

The lowly aspirin does it all: mitigates inflammation, alleviates pain, lowers fevers, thins the blood against possible embolisms, eats away the walls of the stomach, causes intestinal bleeding. And best of all, since none of the drug companies has a monopoly on aspirin, it's as cheap as dirt.

Go to a drug store or a supermarket and head for the aspirin and analgesics section and it's as confusing to the runner as entering a California specialty wine store is to the wine neophyte. Extra strength. Time-release. Buffered. Caffeine-free. Turbo-caffeinated. Gentle on your stomach. 97 octane.

Analgesics (especially aspirin, ibuprofin, and acetaminophen) are staples of the typical runner's kit, especially if the runner is 50 and above, the natural age when aches and pains come with the territory, and where running can alleviate some of them and aggravate others. It is frightening to witness the volume of analgesics runners ingest, seemingly on the theory that, like everything in America, if two are good, four must be better. I've witnessed runners, especially ultrarunners, ingesting literally handfuls of analgesics, with seeming immunity. Unfortunately, this practice can backfire very quickly, and in devastating ways. Runners, especially those over 50, should be attempting to determine how *few* analgesics they can get by with instead of seeing how *many* they can metabolize before, during, or after a run.

On November 26, 1994, Don Davis won the Seagate 100K race in Toledo, Ohio. He was 49 years old at the time and had been running ultras since 1979. Racing against five other runners, Don won in (for him) an easy time of 9:29. Four days later he was hospitalized for 11 days with acute kidney failure. In the hospital the Wednesday after the race, Don faced kidney dialysis if he didn't process fluids during Friday night and early Saturday morning. During Don's race, he had taken 2,400 mg of ibuprofen. "My nephrologists agree that 2,400 mg was too much [ibuprofen] for me, and was a definite contributor to my kidney failure," Don concludes in a three-page report he posted on the World Wide Web.

Dr. Robert Johnson is director of Primary Care Sports Medicine at the Hennepin County Medical Center in Minneapolis and the medical director of the Edmund Fitzgerald 100K Race and Relay. In the January 1997 issue of *Marathon & Beyond* magazine, he wrote an article examining the misuse and overuse of analgesics among marathoners and ultrarunners.

"The use of NSAIDs [Non-Steroidal Anti-Inflammatory Drugs] by athletes has approached mythic proportions, exceeded only by the marketing budgets and retail sales successes of the manufacturers of these drugs. Their [sic] availability over the counter at convenience stores, pharmacies, and grocery stores had only increased their use and overuse with little regard for efficacy or risk," Dr. Johnson concluded. "In fact, I've often referred to these medications as 'Vitamin N' because of their ubiquitous and haphazard use in the athletic community."

Analgesics (including aspirin) are like any other drug: they perform a certain function but not without side effects. And, like any drug, it is especially easy to misuse and overuse them, especially because they are so readily available.

On the plus side, analgesics have a very effective pain-mitigating effect upon the serious runner, especially the runner who runs longer distances and the runner over 50 who is prone to aches and pains the younger runner does not enjoy. Aspirin was originally developed to relieve the pain of arthritis, and it performs that function for the runner who suffers from minor arthritis but who still runs regularly. It is also effective late in a race when old aches and pains divert the runner's concentration from the run or race to the site of the aches; the caution there is to be able to distinguish between an ache and a pain. A regularly-scheduled ache is decidedly different from a stark pain that signals an injury. Use of an analgesic for a pain that points at an oncoming injury will mask the pain signals of the approaching injury and encourage the runner to continue running, thereby compounding the injury. Perhaps the best use of analgesics and aspirin is following a long workout or a race, not to cure chronic aches, but to at least temporarily subdue the pain.

Although in some ways analgesics are the mature runner's friend, like any friend, too much exposure over too long a period of time undermines the benefits of the friendship. As the ancient Greeks used to contend: "Moderation in all things."

Caffeine: Go Juice

Coffeehouses are to the 1990s what video stores were to the 1980s: there's one on every corner. Every small-time entrepreneur thinks a coffeehouse is the way to get into business and make a killing, and gradually a glut forms on the landscape that soon causes the bankruptcy courts to swell with caseloads.

Coffee, long one of America's favorite beverages, has turbocharged itself into a lifestyle ingredient similar to that which it has long enjoyed in Europe. The coffee bars and coffeehouses have added variety to the good old always-brewing American pot o' java at the local diner or the regional trucker's rest.

For many runners, the caffeine in coffee has long been a ritual of the preparation for long runs or long races. Two cups of strong coffee an hour before the run or race supposedly does two very important things: it stimulates a bowel movement (something we more mature runners note with satisfaction) and it stimulates the body's switch from using glycogen to using the much more plentiful free fatty acids as a prime fuel for running.

Of course then there's the other camp, which says that drinking coffee before a race overstimulates the body to its detriment when it comes time to run or race. This process can have every negative effect from causing the runner to go out too fast to stimulating sweating even before the race begins.

Long-running friend Dr. Peter Wood, who until his recent retirement was a professor of medicine at Stanford University, has always had an approach to caffeine (whether it's in coffee, strong tea, cola or other soft drinks, chocolate, whatever) that I find eminently sensible. "You can find whatever kind of research you want when it comes to caffeine," Peter has consistently told me over the past 20 years. "If you want to find a study that says it's bad for you, the study is easy enough to find. And if you want to find a study that says it will do marvelous things for your running, that study is available, too."

In short, there have been literally hundreds of studies done on caffeine, and taking them together, one conclusion can be drawn, and that is: no conclusion can be drawn.

It goes without saying that caffeine is a stimulant. And it is a drug. And as with any drug, it should be respected and used wisely. It is obvious that anyone who drinks more than three cups of coffee a day has a problem—besides the obvious fidgets, that is. Like most drugs presented to the body, there is a usually predictable reaction, but with continued use, the body adapts, and to cause the same reaction in the future, more of the drug must be used. And, as with most drugs, withdrawal from caffeine is difficult. Withdrawal causes headaches, depression, nervousness, a whole host of reactions as the body attempts to readapt to a life without caffeine.

For the mature runner, caffeine, whether in coffee or strong teas, should be treated with respect. Too much strong, acidic coffee can damage the walls of the stomach. Take an aspirin for arthritis or as a prophylactic toward preventing blood clots and wash it down with coffee, and the combination can act like an acid bath on the stomach lining, causing upset stomach and possibly ulceration.

This caution is especially appropriate today, when the specialty coffees we are drinking are so much stronger than the weak coffee that used to be the staple of the American table— you know, the coffee through which you could read a newspaper if you held the pot up to the light. Today's high-octane coffee can be especially harsh on often already-sensitive stomachs. As with aspirin, if you have a sensitive stomach and still want to drink coffee, drink it after or while eating food so there is something to absorb the acidity besides the stomach lining.

As with any other drug, if you are not in the habit of drinking coffee and begin to use it as a training or racing aid, the reaction will be much more profound simply because you are caffeine naive. You may want to water the coffee down or use weakened coffee to moderate the effects. And you may also want to cut it with milk to avoid the gastric effects in the stomach.

Caffeine is also present in fair quantities in many soft drinks, especially colas. Other than Jolt, which bills itself as extremely high in caffeine, the strongest caffeinated soft drink is Mountain Dew. It is also good to keep in mind that quite a few aspirin products contain caffeine. For instance, Extra Strength Excedrin contains a good shot of caffeine.

Because of the combination of caffeine and sugar, some marathoners and ultramarathoners drink defizzed cola or Mountain Dew past the halfway point in their races in order to enjoy that extra stimulation that they feel they need when the fuel tanks seem to be approaching empty. Most ultramarathoners, who are pioneers of eating solid foods while on the run, have some solid foods in their stomachs when they pour in the defizzed cola, which helps mediate the harsh effects on the stomach. Runners who do shorter races typically do not eat solid foods and the process of dumping a can of defizzed cola into a stomach that is already churning out its own acidic juices can be upsetting.

If you are going to use caffeine drinks in your races, it is always advisable to try them out first in training runs in order to determine if you have a negative reaction to them. And begin by using as small a hit of caffeine as you think might work; don't start out with a large quantity and then gradually cut back to the minimum that will work.

Caffeine can have a reviving effect on a runner late in a race, but as with other drugs, we need to respect its potentially negative side.

Alcohol: Moderation in All Things

Most runners know the story of how, to calm his nervousness the night before his 1972 Munich Olympic marathon race,

Frank Shorter drank two liters of German beer. Of course, it is a matter of history that the next day he went on to win the gold medal. Many runners also know of the Hash House Harriers, a fun-loving fraternity of runners with clubs spread all over the world. The Harriers claim to be either a running club with a drinking problem, or a drinking club with a running problem.

And then there are the increasing stacks of studies indicating that two bottles of beer (preferably dark) or two glasses of wine per day are beneficial for the heart. The current studies indicating that moderate alcohol consumption has medicinal properties seem to be a resurrection of theories that are well over 2,000 years old and that permeate ancient civilizations the world over. Alcohol has been used in religious ceremonies for centuries and today wine is even used in some hospitals and nursing homes to stimulate appetite. But, as with any other drug, alcohol in excess is extremely destructive. And, as with other drugs, some people, due to their biological makeup, should avoid it entirely.

For the runner, a moderate amount of alcohol the night before a race or after a race certainly will not hurt. However, the ingestion of excessive amounts of alcohol can undermine running performance. Excessive alcohol can have a negative effect on the oxygen- and nutrient-carrying capacity of the red blood cells.

Alcohol also dehydrates the body, which is the last thing a runner needs the night before a long run or a race when he or she should be hydrating so that the body goes into the long run or race with plenty of fluid onboard. Regular use of alcohol can also have a dehydrating effect on the skin, a concern for older runners, especially those who as reckless youths spent too much time in the sun.

By the time you've passed the 50-year-old landmark, your drinking habits are pretty well set. For improved race results, it would be beneficial to do what world-class marathoner Steve Jones did several weeks before an important race: cut back on alcohol consumption in order to give the blood the opportunity to maximize its all-important oxygen-carrying capacity.

Although "one for the road" has taken on new meaning in the wake of recent research, a little moderation goes a long way.

Endorphins: The Natural High

The subject of the fabled "runner's high" has been fraught with controversy. Serious runners have long contended that there is no such thing, while more casual runners have long contended that it is real. The schism is easily explained by the angle from which each group of runners approaches the sport, according to William Glasser in his groundbreaking book, *Positive Addiction.*

© Terry Wild Studio

According to Glasser, under certain conditions (such as long-distance running), the brain releases endorphins or natural opiates, which impart a feeling of well-being. The theory is that the endorphins were a protective device in primitive mankind against being slowed down or hobbled by minor injuries and discomforts while in pursuit of animals to provide food for the tribe. While in pursuit of game, the endorphins would kick in and mask minor cuts, scrapes, fatigue, and so on, in order to give the hunter more of a chance to pull off a successful hunt.

Glasser found in his studies that national- and world-class runners did not report experiencing this endorphin release. He theorized that while the endorphins were probably being released, the top-drawer athlete did not perceive their effects because the top-drawer athlete is used to training in a self-critical manner. That is, in a mode of constantly monitoring the function—or dis-function—of body systems in order to run at a maximum level. Less serious runners, on the other hand, perceived the runner's high because they were less critical of their running and therefore more open to whatever happened during their runs. Although endorphins are likely released during every long run, the "high" they produce may not be recognized unless the run is going particularly smoothly.

The presence of the endorphins and the subsequent feeling of well-being they engender may play a major role in how human beings can not only stick with, but relish an activity such as running which, by all logic, should eventually peak out as the height of boredom: one foot in front of the other, then alternate.

Certainly there are other factors on the side of running that contribute to its ongoing appeal. But the endorphin-fed equanimity one receives from running regularly cannot be discounted as a prime factor in so many people running for so many years that they continue to do it into their fifth, sixth, and seventh decades of life.

For the 50+ runner, the positive effects of a regular dose of endorphins cannot be discounted as a contributor to ongoing health, fitness, and well-being.

PART

IV

Training Alone and Together

13

Sharing

*"It is one of the most
beautiful compensations of this
life that no man can sincerely
try to help another without
helping himself."*

—Ralph Waldo Emerson

For many runners, there has been a sea change when it comes to running as a group: a change from running in a group to compete with each other and thereby improve one's running, to running in a group to socialize. This is especially evident among two types of runners: mature runners who regularly train together several times a week and younger female runners who are entering the sport in increasing numbers and who train together in groups for safety and mutual support. This process literally places the running second to the socializing and, in the process, more thoroughly integrates running into the daily routine because the competitive pressure to perform at a certain level is removed from the running.

Translation, please.

During the late 1970s and early 1980s, many runners hooked up with other runners on a regular basis to do strenuous workouts. Typically, the runs started out benignly enough as the runners worked the kinks out, warmed up, became smoother, and picked up the pace. As often as not, once everyone was warmed up, one or the other runner would further pick up the pace and the rest would go with him. If, in the process, one or two of the runners dropped back, so be it. The group run was a great excuse to improve by essentially re-creating a race situation in which runners sparred back and forth, in the process becoming better running animals.

A fair number of world-class female runners who in this period catapulted women's running onto the next level of performance were in the habit of regularly training with groups of male runners, in the process closing the gap between how male runners trained and how female runners might train to improve faster.

RUTH ANDERSON

It would be difficult to find a runner of either sex or any age who has exhibited the range Ruth Anderson has over her 25-year career.

Now approaching 70 years old, Ruth, a former scientist at the Lawrence Livermore Labs in Livermore, California, in 1978 set a track record of 2:45 at 800 meters and in 1986 set a 24-hour track record of 110.5 miles in the 55–59 age group that still stands today. Over her splendid career she's run more than 70 ultramarathon events and 102 marathons.

But Ruth's contribution to running has not merely been to the record books. She has untiringly worked behind the scenes to advance the roles and opportunities of women in running. She has contributed time and energy in the administration and organization of masters running, for which service she received national awards from the USATF (USA Track and Field) for meritorious service in 1977, 1984, and 1991. She broke ground for women in ultrarunning by working behind the scenes to open the famed London-to-Brighton 54.25-mile ultra to women; in 1979 she became the first woman to be officially allowed to run the race and finished as third woman overall—at age 50!

She also worked behind the scenes on various long-distance committees to bring the first women's Olympic marathon to fruition. In 1991 she earned the USATF Distinguished Achievement Award from the USATF Women's Long Distance Running Committee for her contributions toward establishing an Olympic marathon for women.

In 1980 Ruth and Boston Marathon winner Nina Kuscsik became the first females to be inducted into the Road Runners Club of America Hall of Fame. In 1997 she was inducted into the USATF's Masters Hall of Fame.

In 1978 she won the *Runner's World* Nurmi Award as Best USA Woman Masters Runner and Best USA Woman Ultramarathoner.

Since turning 50 in 1979, Ruth has literally been an age-group record-making machine at a variety of distances and disciplines. In 1979 she won the 50–54 age-group WAVA (World Association of Veteran Athletes) marathon championships in Hanover, Germany with a 3:15; at the same meet she won her age group in the cross-country championships. In 1983 she won her age group in the WAVA cross-country championships in Puerto Rico. In 1984 she won her age group in the IGAL (a German forerunner of WAVA concerned only with road racing) marathon championships marathon in San Diego with a 3:23. In 1985 she won the 50–54 age-group title in the IGAL 25K championships in England.

Her national championship age-group titles literally take up pages. A few highlights:

- 1988 100K championships in Minnesota: 11:56:23
- 1980 50-mile championships in Houston: 7:10:23
- 1985 50K cross-country championships in California: 5:35:37
- 1994 marathon championships in Minnesota: 4:11:56
- 1985 30K championships in Texas: 2:22:29
- 1992 25K championships in California: 2:22:53
- 1989 20K championships in Oregon: 1:39:08

- 1980 15K championships in Washington: 1:03:12
- 1989 10K cross-country championships in California: 54:57
- 1982 5-mile championships in Pennsylvania: 35:05
- 1989 8K championships in Washington, DC: 38:48
- 1995 5K championships in Carlsbad (Calif.): 26:14

In 1997 Ruth traveled to Durban, South Africa, to take part in the WAVA XII Championships, which kept her string alive of having competed at all 12 world championships. Although she used to compete in everything from the 800 meters to the marathon at the world veterans' games, she now confines herself to the 10K cross-country race and the marathon. In the cross-country race she placed fifth overall in the W65–69 women's competition; she and teammates Lee Glascco (65 years old) and Louise Adams (75) won the silver for team placement. She also won the bronze medal in the marathon in the W65–69 age group.

Ruth, along with a handful of other marathoners, took great pains to run a few extra marathons during 1995 in order to go into the 1996 "100th" Boston Marathon as her 100th career marathon, where she ran 4:40:42.

She is also a great organizer of teams of older runners who enter relay events. Since 1987 she has been the captain of a Lake Merritt Joggers & Striders team at the Lake Tahoe (Calif.) Relays. The average age of the 1997 team was 55-1/2 years of age.

Ruth more than qualifies as the classic overachiever, but after 25 years of running well in more races than the average runner enters in a lifetime, her enthusiasm for the sport and the people comes through brightly and is contagious.

She bubbles over with enthusiasm for the sport and lifestyle of running and infects everyone she encounters with the running bug. "I don't know another activity that's easier to do or that rewards people so immediately and so directly," she said. "I feel privileged to have met so many wonderful people through running, so many people with whom I've stayed friends for literally decades. People who run some of these outrageous distances are very special, very motivated people. Many of them say that my achievements in the sport have inspired them, but it's they who inspire me. There is absolutely no doubt in my mind that running has greatly enhanced and colored my life like a freshly-minted rainbow. It always gives back so much more than you put into it."

During this period, some of us went so far as to once a week schedule a run with a group that was significantly faster than we were in an effort to become better racers. We'd run a few warm-up miles, then run the first several miles with the studs while they warmed the kinks out of their legs. Even though we were warmed up, we still had trouble holding the pace while the good runners merely loosened up. When the pace became too much for us, we'd drop back and fall into a more comfortable pace we could hold through the completion of the workout. But we had, for a few miles at least, run with our betters and in the process we became better for it.

Group Run for Fun

This process of improvement by road test still goes on today, but there has also been a major shift when it comes to running with groups that is refreshing and encouraging to novice runners, average runners, and older runners. It is a tendency for groups to run at the speed of the slowest member which, for the older runner, can be a godsend in that such group runs can serve to place a governor on a runner to prevent him or her from running too fast and hard when it isn't called for on that day's schedule.

This type of group running is nonintimidating, even encouraging, and in many instances has kept veteran runners involved in the sport long after they might have fallen out the other end, if for no other reason than they traded addiction to competition to addiction to the social nature of the runs.

Social running has been the salvation of many a runner who has been running almost mechanically for decades or who competed heavily at one time and began to burn out. Although it is impossible to separate the runner from the run, and all runs are technically done alone because no one else can do our runs for us, social running can save a flagging running career—and has been responsible for launching literally tens of thousands of running and racing careers.

Some runners would not be running at all if it weren't for a special group of running partners who motivate each other to get in the miles, come rain or shine. There is an increasing tendency for social running these days because of the number of running classes and running store sponsored training groups that are formed to build toward certain racing goals, such as running a first marathon. In many instances, a training group is formed and even after the goal of the group is reached, a nucleus of the group finds that it has bonded to the extent that those runners continue to run as a group for years afterwards and even travel to distant races together.

Benefits of Group Running

The benefits of running with a group, especially for mature runners, are numerous:

• Runners within a regular running group cajole and encourage each other to make a commitment to step out the door and get in the miles, even if it involves laying down a little guilt on each other: no excuses or you'll be letting down the group. This is especially effective with older runners, who appear to be more thoroughly grounded in the motivating force inherent in guilt than most younger people are today.

• While in a group, there is a tendency to interact socially, to hold long convoluted conversations while on the run, instead of concentrating on the miles to be run that day; as a result, the miles melt away with seeming ease and the workout is over almost before it begins. This is additionally beneficial for the runner who needs to be reminded to keep most runs slow and steady enough so as to be at a conversational pace.

• Members of a running group feed off each other. There is a nondenominational energy-sharing phenomenon that becomes apparent when running with a group, a passing back and forth of group energy when it is needed by a specific member. Anyone who has regularly run with the same group begins to pick up on this exchange of energy, a phenomenon in which the total energy of the group seems to be greater than the total sum of the energy of the individuals. For runners with

© Terry Wild Studio

a great many miles on their legs, this "reserve fuel tank" phenomenon is extremely refreshing, a new lease on life.

• There is safety in numbers. A running group, whether primarily female or older runners, can run in places and at times when a lone runner would feel insecure and at risk. This safety factor is encouraging to older runners and tends to add a feeling of confidence to the run while also contributing to the relaxation within the run.

• There is a special form of bonding that occurs in a running group that is impossible to achieve in any other situation. This is especially valuable for older runners who sometimes feel cut loose socially after the children leave home or old friends move away or die, and there is no longer the social structure available for easily developing new friendships. The process of jointly taking part in an ongoing physical activity raises social intercourse to a unique level. Many runners have developed a very special space in their lives for their running group, yet that special space exists only during the process of running. In some instances, the special bonding does not extend beyond the group run, and each member of the group respects that special bond and they refuse to jeopardize it by pushing it outside the running.

• In a world where we are becoming more fractionalized along ethnic, gender, and age lines, the typical running group is usually above such distinctions. Although most running groups tend to be somewhat homogeneous, that commonality is sometimes based not on age or sex or race or political persuasion but on average training pace. As a result, the running group can provide a regular social structure in which members of society that would seldom find themselves inter-acting with each other are thrown together, with often delight-ful cross-generational and cross-gender results.

• Goals of improving one's running that are established democratically by the group can often be achieved more easily as a group than on one's own. This is almost profoundly true when the group decides to tackle a particularly challenging goal, such as training for a marathon. Training alone for a marathon can be intimidating; training with a group makes the goal seem not only possible, but even enjoyable, no matter one's previous running achievements or age.

• The previous benefit especially extends to doing speed or track workouts. Runners who would never consider going to a track to do speed workouts on their own often find the process actually enjoyable when they do it as part of a once-a-week track group that, following the workout, goes out for pizza or gathers at one of the member's homes to extend the workout by comparing notes and talking out the workouts while also planning next week's goals.

Although running is, by its nature, an individual sport and activity, the running group is a concept that has been with us since the hemerodromi of classic Greece trained together toward their profession as message carriers. It was with us in the 1970s as the Florida Track Club trained together and produced outstanding runners such as Frank Shorter, Jeff Galloway, Jack Bacheler, and Kenny Moore. It is with us today as older runners regularly get together for a few (or many) miles and some shared experience. And it will be with us tomorrow, as more and more running groups are organized specifically for training toward common goals.

If you have not made a connection with a regular training group, consider contacting your local Road Runners Club of America chapter. Check the activities section of your local newspaper, or contact the RRCA at 1150 S. Washington St., Ste. 250, Alexandria, VA 22314, 703-836-0558, fax 703-836-4430, e-mail RRCAOffice@rrca.org, or check them out on the Web at **http://rrca.org.**

Aloning

*"One man with courage
is a majority."*

—Andrew Jackson

Of all the millions of feet of mental running film I have stored in my brain from decades of putting one foot in front of the other, there is one image that persists above all others, and not only because in real life it was repeated on a daily basis. That image is of the late (and great) bare- and barrel-chested Walt Stack running across the Golden Gate Bridge in the early morning fog.

A grizzled labor organizer from the 1930s, a hard-working hod carrier well into his 60s, Walt Stack came to running late in life. But what a life he brought to it—and what an impact he had on his adopted sport. Known fondly as The Ancient Marathoner, Walt was a character straight out of central casting: sun-tanned chest the size and shape of a 55-gallon drum, piercing glacier-blue eyes, a personal history writ in tattoos long before they emerged from back alleys into popular culture.

Walt was for years president of the Dolphin South End Running Club, whose motto was (and still is) "Start slowly ... and then taper off." During his tenure, Walt Stack probably did more than any other running club president in the world to encourage women runners, older runners, minority runners, nonrunners, burned out runners, fun runners, back-of-the-pack runners. Today, the DSE Running Club remains the most diverse running club in the world.

When Walt Stack ran a race, he was surrounded by his adoring and incredibly diverse fans. Proto-feminists loved Walt because he encouraged them in their running and told them they could do anything they set their minds to. For Walt's 75th birthday, a special 10K race was organized in San Francisco by the runners he'd brought into the sport. A small army of women who wore business suits all week created short-cut togas for themselves that would have looked more at home at a Greek bacchanalia than a footrace, and with Walt safely tucked in the middle of their adoring group they literally ran the 10K race while cooling him with waving palm fronds.

The crowd-pleasing, crowd-inspiring, mega-social Walt Stack ran most of his training miles completely and deliciously alone. But there are a fair number of runners today—especially runners new to the sport—who seldom, if ever, run alone. For them, running is and must be a group activity. The very motivation to get out the door and run comes from fellow runners, the regularly-scheduled run is a social event, and the running partner or group provides the anchor or focus of the individual's running.

WALT STACK

To call Walt Stack a colorful character would be to underuse the phrase. Walt Stack was one of those "colorful characters" the city of San Francisco has traditionally produced when he or she was needed. For many years, as Walt made his daily run across the Golden Gate Bridge bare-chested and tattooed, no matter what the weather, he drew more attention from commuters making their way into the fog-bound city than the bridge itself.

Walt's daily training routine was legendary. He'd rise around 3 A.M. and ride his doddering one-speed bicycle to the Dolphin Swim Club on the edge of the San Francisco Bay, where he'd park the old clunker. Then he'd run out to the Golden Gate Bridge and across it down into Sausalito, where he'd turn around and return to the Dolphin Swim Club. His next leg was to leap into the bitter chill of the San Francisco Bay, paddle around for a half-hour, come back to the swim club, sit in the sauna to warm up, then hop back on his bicycle to get to work. Work for Walt was hod carrier: a human machine that carried 50–60 pounds of wet cement up a ladder on a construction site to make it available to the bricklayers. Walt worked as a hod carrier well beyond what is considered retirement age.

His daily routine during the 1970s trained him well for the emerging sport of the triathlon. The only year he entered the Hawaii Ironman, he rode his antiquated one-speed bicycle while everyone else in the field was pushing hi-tech. In his typical salty summation of the experience, he remarked that "I've been on that damned bike so long they're gonna have to surgically remove the seat from my ass."

Walt's salty jokes and stories were about as politically incorrect as they came in the late '70s and early '80s, and in a liberal-leaning city like San Francisco it could be assumed that the crusty old reprobate would have been a pariah.

On the contrary. Walt was the delight of female runners in San Francisco. As

exalted leader of the Dolphin South End Running Club—the running arm of the Dolphin Swim Club, the South End Rowing Club, and the San Francisco Rowing Club—Walt encouraged everyone to run, especially women. He was the cheerleader for every woman who was willing to lace on a pair of running shoes and take to the roads. He annually took busloads of women to the grueling Pike's Peak Marathon—women he had convinced they could do the race, women he had coached and cajoled into tapping into their physical sides toward broadening their lives.

When Walt ran in marathons, he traveled at a consistent 8:00–9:00 pace. He once commented on his pace: "I've been running eight-minute miles so long that if I fell out of an airplane, I'd fall at eight minutes a mile." He was constantly surrounded by other runners, mostly women, who hung onto his ceaseless ribald joke-telling. At one point he claimed that he got roughly four miles per beer. A fan built him a leather holster that held six cans of beer to get him within striking distance of the marathon finish line.

His club held—and still holds—informal races every Sunday. During Walt's day, the entry fee was 50 cents and every participant received a ribbon. The club was—and is—the most diversified running club in the world, echoing Walt's view that everyone, anyone can run.

For Walt's 75th birthday, a celebration was staged on the Liberty ship Jeremiah O'Brien. The mayor declared the day "Walt Stack Day." A special 10K birthday run was held during which Walt was escorted by an entourage of prominent women runners wearing white nymph-like costumes while waving palm leaves. Walt's speech was, as usual, peppered with salty dog references and jokes. At one point, he looked out to Alcatraz Island, where he had at one time been incarcerated for going AWOL from the army when he was 15, and said, "What a wonderful country. In one decade they put me in jail out there in the middle of the bay and a few decades later they're declaring I have my own day."

When Walt died, his beloved Dolphin South End Running Club declared him "president angelicus." In 1995 his club instituted the Walt Stack Trail 25K, which follows the course of his daily run across the Golden Gate Bridge to Sausalito and back.

For many in the Bay Area who commute across the Golden Gate Bridge, a foggy day can lead to Walt sightings. Just out of the corner of the driver's eye, there is barrel-chested, bare-chested, tattooed, icy-blue-eyed Walt, shuffling across the bridge, acknowledging with a wave each driver who toots his horn.

The Ancient Marathoner, a man who started running late in life and who never won a race but never met a race he didn't love, has become the immortal legend of San Francisco running.

Yet, as stated in the previous chapter, every run taken is an individual enterprise, even if it is in the company of 29,000 other runners in the New York City Marathon or with more than 60,000 others in a mega-race like the San Francisco Bay-to-Breakers or Spokane's Bloomsday Race.

For a fair number of runners, especially older runners who are the possessors of sometimes too-full lives, their solo run provides a form of therapy, a ritual of renewal that they jealously guard as their special "alone" time. "Alone" and "lonely" are not, of course, synonymous. For runners blessed with busy lives, their hour of running alone is precious and carefully protected because it is the anchor that holds every other directive in life at bay.

It is worth considering the formidable pros of running alone:

• You run when and where you want. You are independent, free of fitting your running into other people's schedules. If you get the urge to run earlier or later than usual, there is no running partner or group with whom you've got to check. If, in the middle of a run, you decide to cut it short or extend it or turn it in a radically different direction, you need not worry about how it is going to affect anyone else. This is especially valuable for older runners who, after a lifetime of fulfilling pressing responsibilities, now relish a bit of independence.

• You set your own pace for the run, or you can change the pace whenever you wish. When you run with a group, you run a pace set by the group, often by its slowest member. If you happen to hit a point in the run where you are feeling good and would like to drop the pace by 30 seconds per mile, you can do just that if you're running alone, and do not have to worry or feel guilty about leaving the group or going against its dictates. For the older runner who is running to his or her own drummer, this freedom is hard-won and appreciated.

• When you run alone, you can clear your head without distractions. When you run with a group, there is usually a fair amount of chatter, which can be interesting, but which is also distracting. One of the reviving aspects of running is the process whereby, when you run alone, the day's problems and worries fall away one by one until everything in life seems extremely simple. Vexing problems that seemed very much like the Gordian Knot are loosened with each stride until the answer is revealed to be the height of simplicity, until you wonder to yourself, "Now why didn't I think of that earlier? . . ." You didn't think of it earlier because your life was cluttered and you needed to get away from the clutter by running alone, by allowing the run to settle into its sublime simplistic self where complexities don't exist. On a group run, this process doesn't occur, and oh, the loss.

© Ken Lee

• A group run tends to pull all members of the group through while a solo run allows you the opportunity to work on your own personal fortitude by pushing through those occasional workouts that actually require work to complete. The process of knowing yourself by testing yourself is valuable at all levels of life, but is especially valuable if it can be performed in the context of your runs—especially if you are in the habit of racing. The Greeks urged each other to "know thyself." On a solo run, the process is simplified and fortified, and the opportunity to "know thyself" is ever-present. For the 50+ runner, these runs are revelations—and character-builders.

• Training alone, especially on a long run, is excellent practice for racing. There are numerous distractions on a group run. On a long solo run, you can hear the steady bellows of your lungs, you can chart the rhythm of your stride, you can monitor various body functions without interruption or distraction, and by doing so, become a better runner and racer. By doing this alone, older runners, sometimes sensitive about having lost some of their basic speed with age, can build it back in a very noncritical environment.

• On the flip side, on a long solo run that is not designed for any specific purpose, you can disassociate much more easily than you can on a group run, just allowing your mind to spin out and get in sync with the course and with the varying degrees of your effort. A two-hour run where you can allow your mind to sail along is worth 10 hours of therapy on a psychiatrist's couch.

Considering the number of runners, especially mature runners, plying the roads and trails of America today, the fabled "loneliness of the long-distance runner" seems to be long gone. It isn't. And it will never be, especially when we consider the irony of the title of the famed novel, wherein the lead character found in his runs the only shreds of freedom he enjoyed all day.

chapter

15

Inspiring

*"I believe that we each have a
responsibility to influence those around
us. Whether we know it or not, we are
influencing them anyway. I just like to
make a conscious decision to do it for the positive."*

—Helen Klein

Running with a group or running alone would seem to effectively cover all possibilities. Running, being the incredibly simple sport that it is, keeps our choices—and our lives—simple: alone or with a partner or group.

But there is a third possibility that is rich in potential but that surprisingly few consider, a third possibility that offers deep mines of inspiration for our personal running. That area involves volunteerism: volunteerism at races, with local school programs, and with local running clubs.

We can only go within ourselves so often for inspiration to fuel our running. For most runners, the personal inspiration for running comes from a deep psychological well, but one that is not bottomless. Too frequently runners become self-absorbed with their own running to the extent that they close out the many other aspects of the sport. When that happens, it is like taking a fateful turn down a lonesome road where we missed the warning sign that this is Not A Through Road. The longer we've been running with psychological blinders on, the nearer the end of the road we are, and the nearer the end of getting the most out of running.

The June Renewal

One of the high points on the running calendar each year for a group of us from Northern California is not a run or a race we personally do. Instead, it is our annual volunteer duty at an aid station out in the middle of the wilderness in support of the Western States Trail 100 Endurance Run the last weekend of June.

© Ken Lee

Quite a few of the hardy volunteers at our aid station are veterans of the Western States 100. Some of us are runners who've done some less-than-sane running in our careers but who have never done the Western States 100. Others are barely runners. Some have never run. But each year we come together to form an aid station that is remote and barely accessible, but that is an opportunity for a wonderful renewal of our passion for the sport and that infuses our personal running for months following.

The first few years we manned what is known as the California #3 aid station, which is about as remote as it gets. It is located at the fork of two badly-tilted dirt roads halfway up the side of a river valley. The terrain is so tight that only five four-wheel-drive trucks can be taken in to the station, and those five can barely be turned around to come back out. But the aid station is at the 72-mile point of the race, where the competitors are in need of fluids, food, occasionally medical attention, and sometimes being pointed in the right direction so they don't get lost in the middle of the night.

In more recent years, we've been reassigned to what is known as Red Star Ridge, a remote open area along a ridgeline at about 7,200 feet at the 17-mile point of the race. We have more than a dozen volunteers at Red Star Ridge, a station so early in the race that we drive to it the night before the race and camp out so we're up and organized by 5:00 A.M. In 1995 the snow from the previous winter was still so deep by June that the roads were impassable, and water and six members of our aid station had to be helicoptered in to the spot to provide basic services.

From what does the inspiration for one's own running come by volunteering? Quite simply from three sources:

• *Contributing to facilitating the intrepid athletes* in reaching their race goals is extremely satisfying. It's an inspiration to see the runners in the top spots come dashing through your aid station, especially since at a typical race, once the starter's gun goes off, that's the last most of us ever see of them—unless we're on an out-and-back course. But it is an inspiration to see—and assist—the middle-of-the-packers and especially the runners in one's own age group. In ultrarunning, the race often goes to the most wily and not merely the fastest, and some of the runners in our 50+ age groups are past masters in pacing themselves to incredible performances. Of course in the case of the Western States 100, there is a tremendous difference in the condition of the athletes at 17 miles (Red Star) and at 72 miles (California #3). But being an integral witness and, in fact, a contributing factor to their success is an inspiration to want to get out there and do it yourself.

• *Working in concert with* instead of in competition with fellow runners is also inspirational. In race situations, we are usually in pursuit of our own goals and dreams, but in the process we are also competing with others, whether or not we intend to. In working an aid station or in some other way volunteering to work at a race, there is a tremendous sense of pulling together as a team to make everything as smooth and safe as possible for the runners. This is especially true at an aid station like Red Star, which is still relatively early in the race, and where the aid station team works together to at times fill the water bottles of two dozen runners at once as they descend on the station in waves. The experience is much like being in the middle of an episode of *M*A*S*H*, and in fact at times has been very much like that, especially at California #3 on a hot afternoon and evening when runners come stumbling in dehydrated, blistered, disoriented, and occasionally in real medical danger. The sense of everyone pulling together is invigorating—especially after all the runners have safely gone through and the crew can breathe a sigh of relief.

• *Being an integral part of the overall race.* Whether it's the Western States 100, the New York City Marathon, or the local 10K road race and walk that benefits a charity, it is inspirational and uplifting to be part of the organization that successfully puts on an event that benefits others. No matter whether you're the person who cleans up the paper cups after the runners have gone through an aid station or you are the aid station captain or the assistant race director, the sense of cooperatively pulling off a successful event infuses your own running for weeks following—as do the occasional snippets of memory of specific runners going through your station. The electricity that comes from being a part of the bigger picture is a feeling that fades only gradually—if at all.

Joining a Team

Whether we run mostly alone or with a partner or a group, running is essentially an individual enterprise. No one else can put in our training and racing miles for us. Yet running as a team sport is becoming more and more popular, especially as running friends put teams together to do marathons or to take part in well-established ultra-long relay events such as the Hood-to-the-Coast Relays in Oregon.

Yet there is an area where running has always been a team sport: in the local high schools and colleges that have track and cross-country teams.

I found it curious when I ran cross-country in college in Pennsylvania in the 1960s that the coach of the Cheyney State College cross-country team actually ran with his runners! Gad, we thought, the guy's in his 30s and he's training with his team! How bizarre!

High school and college cross-country coaches and assistant coaches running with their teams isn't as weird as it used to be. In fact, it is becoming relatively common. My younger brother, who is now 50, coaches high school cross-country in Pennsylvania and he runs with his team. On those occasions when I get back to Pennsylvania to visit, I find myself looking forward to the opportunity to run with his team.

When I first did it years ago, they were astonished that "older people" could not only run, but on several instances, run farther than high school runners could. But more importantly, once we were all several miles into the run and warmed up, as usually happens, groups who are doing approximately the same pace form and suddenly all age barriers are gone, and it's just a group of runners out on a workout. Everyone relaxes, the banter goes back and forth, the camaraderie gets as thick as Shoe-Goo, and there is no generational divide—other than the occasional historical reference points in the conversations, many of which involve astonishment on their part that you were actually alive when certain historic events took place, such as when JFK was killed or when the Beatles invaded America.

When running with high school cross-country runners, it's impossible to not pick up their enthusiasm and energy. And, from their conversations and concerns, to not pick up on the fact that over time, very little changes. The concerns of today's teenagers may be phrased and articulated differently, but they are essentially the same concerns we had when we were teenagers, which were probably the same our grandparents had when they were teens.

Volunteering at your local high school to be an assistant track or cross-country coach could help the financially strapped school while giving your own running a tremendous shot in the leg. And in the process, you'll be astonished at what you can learn from these dedicated younger people, while perhaps they can learn something from you.

On the Club Beat

Local running clubs are the backbone of running in America. Many of the races you attend are put on by running clubs. In some areas, running trails and courses are maintained by the local running clubs. Running clubs put on clinics and group runs and track training get-togethers. Many running clubs also offer age-group subsets within their organizations to encourage and foster running among veteran runners.

If you are a veteran runner, there is no easier way to hook up with other veteran runners than by joining your local running club. There is also no better way to have your enthusiasm and motivation regularly infused. Clubs put together age-group relay teams, enter age-group teams in regional competitions, and promote age-group awards in local races.

It is probably axiomatic that in every organization, 20 percent of the members do 80 percent of the work. Certainly it's no different in running clubs. There is no running club that cannot use volunteer help, especially when it is offered by a mature, responsible runner. And there is no quicker way for a mature runner to enjoy personal satisfaction within the larger running community than to direct some of the time and energy you have available toward promoting running.

As I write this chapter in late 1996, the Road Runners Club of America has divided California into two halves (as some of us California residents would like to see it divided politically . . .), and state representatives have been appointed to coordinate the two halves of the state. Norm Haines of Big Bear City is now the Southern California rep; he's 57 years old, owns a property management company, and is president and newsletter editor of the Big Bear Running Club, as well as race director of the Big Bear Classic 5K and 10K; he also makes time to train for and run ultras.

In Northern California, Mariposa "Po" Adams of Carmichael is the new rep. Po has long been a member of the Buffalo Chips Running Club in Sacramento, and is a spokesperson for the Senior Games and a member of the Governor's Council on Sports and Fitness. She's 72 years old, has run races all over the world, and in early 1996, when she failed to qualify for the "100th" running of Boston, she flew 3,000 miles to help out as a volunteer!

For many mature runners, running does become a bit more than merely putting one foot in front of the other and alternating.

PART

The Walking Wounded

Avoiding

*"Small opportunities are often
the beginning of great enterprises."*

—Demosthenes

I am occasionally filled with concern when it comes to inviting nonrunners and runners to the same party. Not that I have a lot of nonrunning friends who smoke cigarettes, spit on the floor, or disrupt the prevailing discourse of the day by injecting politics, religion, or philosophies of raising kids to spoil the party.

My concern centers more on the confusion the nonrunning folks must take home with them in the wake of an afternoon and evening hearing about the "injuries" runners suffer. A few days after one such party several years ago, I bumped into one of the nonrunning guests at a supermarket and was amused to be asked this: "Are all of your friends accident-prone? All they do is talk about getting injured. . . ."

For most runners, injury is an occupational hazard, as we'll see in the next chapter. Certainly it is a truism that as we age as runners, we become more prone to injuries—especially to injuries that we've already supposedly put behind us. An old injury is like a rock bruise on the windshield of a car: it is primed to expand at the least urging.

But as we age, we are also theoretically wiser, which means that we should have learned by now that there are certain tried and true methods of avoiding running injuries. And, it goes without saying, that this is also a truism: the best injury to have is the one you avoided.

It is worthwhile to review the Seven Commandments of Injury Avoidance:

Always Warm Up Before a Run

Running on cold muscles is like racing a car engine immediately upon starting it up on a cold morning. There is nothing good that happens within the engine as stiff, unoiled parts scrape against each other. Similarly with the body's moving parts. To go rushing out the door on a run is to invite injury. And the older we get, the stiffer we get, so the more prone we are to becoming injured if we start out too fast before the muscles and ligaments are warmed up.

If you are beginning a run on a particularly cold morning, walk a few blocks to get the stiffness out, then roll into a very easy shuffle. Give your muscles a chance to loosen up and to become a bit more supple before making demands upon them. Use the first 15 minutes as warm-up, jogging gently until the muscles massage themselves into looseness and the blood is flowing freely.

Naturally, on a warm or hot day, the warm-up can be shortened because the air temperature is going to do some of the work for you. Treat your body gently and with respect before asking it to perform at a high level.

Always Follow a Hard Day With Two or More Easy Days

The surest way to court injury is to run too hard too long or too hard too often. Even college-age runners can be overworked by doing too many hard workouts within a week. Good running coaches are able to determine by working closely with a runner just how much time he or she needs to come back from a hard workout. It was not unusual even in the 1970s to have college coaches increase the

number of easy days following a hard day for some of their charges.

The situation is exaggerated for runners as they get older. As we've discussed before, there is not a rapid drop-off of workouts an older runner can pull off. But there is an increasing need for more recovery time. Too much hard work without necessary recovery (and each runner is individual and unique when it comes to how much recovery time is needed) will lead to injury.

Schedule One or Two Rest Days per Week

Although some runners pride themselves on not having missed a day in their running for the past 10 or 15 or even 20 years, for most of us, running seven days a week is a sure route to early retirement from the sport.

As stated in #2, as we age we need more recovery time. Recovery time can come in one of two forms: easy workouts following hard workouts, or rest days. We should schedule at least one full rest day into our weekly workout schedule, and for some of us two days of complete rest from physical activities. Other older runners will be able to get away with one full rest day and a semi-rest day per week. The semi-rest day may involve some other aerobic activity or strength-training exercise.

Keep a journal to track the results of your hard workouts, easy workouts, and rest days. Pay attention to how quickly or how slowly you recover from a hard workout and adjust your schedule accordingly.

It is important to realize that even on a day of absolute, luxurious rest, you are still training: your body is working to recover from its last hard workout. Ignore the need for rest and injury will be your constant companion.

Undergo a Deep-Tissue Massage at Least Once a Month

World-class runners receive regular sports massage sessions in order to extend their careers. Many have a deep-tissue massage two or three times a week to break up the formation of scar tissue. Those of us who do not make our living by running against other world-class athletes can learn something from those runners.

Even if you've never done it before, track down a competent sports masseur and go for an hour session. Local running stores and running clubs usually know the best massage therapists in the area. Don't just go to someone who does massage. Make certain it's a sports masseur. And don't make them guess where you're hurting and need work. Explain your running routine, detail chronic injuries, point out body locations that are currently feeling sore or stiff.

Don't plan to do a hard workout the day after a deep-tissue sports massage. And don't expect the massage to be fun. The good sports massage therapist will work you over pretty well, and may hit some especially sensitive or sore spots that need some diligent work.

Although they aren't cheap, good sports massage therapists are plenty cheaper than sports medicine doctors who attempt to put the pieces back together after you've injured yourself. The sports massage therapist can be the older runner's single best partner in extending a satisfying running career. This comes from a gradually won-over convert who long harbored doubts as to the effectiveness of such therapy.

If You Stretch, Do It Carefully and Properly

It may come as a shock to advocates of stretching, but there was a study of 4,000 injured runners by podiatrist Dr. John Pagliano released in 1996 that indicated that the third most common cause of running injuries was stretching. This comes as a shocker because stretching advocates have long asserted that stretching *prevents running injuries.*

Of course, there has always been a hard-core cult of runners who have asserted literally for decades that stretching was bad for you, that they never did it, that it went counter to the process of running, and that they would take great pains to avoid stretching. The reality probably lies somewhere in between.

My own impression of stretching has always been one of alarm. Wandering around and through a throng of runners warming up on a chilly morning at 6:50 A.M. for a 7:00 A.M. race, I'd find myself wincing at the sight of seemingly perfectly sane people placing the heel of their shoe on the bumper of a car and then stretching their leg out parallel to the ground, after which acrobatics, they'd begin to bob their head forward until eventually their forehead would touch their knee. Ouch! I could imagine cold muscle fibers screaming out in pain as they were pulled asunder all the way up and down the back of the leg. That, I thought to myself, can't be good for you. So I'd confine my warm-up to jogging slowly around the parking lot.

There are, of course, all kinds of stretching, and all kinds of stretching "experts," some of whom actually warn people against stretching a cold muscle. For runners, it is much safer to gently jog a mile or two to warm up the working muscles before doing gentle static (nonbouncing) stretching. Observe a cat. You never see a cat doing ballistic (bouncing) stretching. If, during a stretch, you feel any discomfort, back off on the stretch.

It is also logical to save your stretching for after your normal running workout, when the muscles are well-warmed and are more likely to accommodate the stretching movements. The exception would be at the end of a long or hard workout, when the muscles have gone through the warmed-up phase and progressed over the edge into the tightened-up stage from being stressed too much.

The best stretching routine I know of is done by long-time running friend Joe Oakes, a guy who's done everything from the Western States 100 and the Ironman Triathlon to 400-meter sprints. Joe does his daily 10 minutes of gentle stretching before he gets out of bed, while he's still warm from six hours of sleeping under warm covers. Which may account for his longevity. In late 1996, Joe celebrated 50 years of running.

JOE OAKES

There's not a horizon that hasn't lured Joe Oakes off the straight and narrow. A runner for most of his life, Joe has competed in everything from the 200 meters to the Western States 100 and multi-day races, sometimes very well, sometimes not so well.

Lured by the philosophy that we only go around once in life, more than a decade ago Joe wound down his business interests and set up his life to give himself options. One of his options was in 1978 to found the Fat Ass Fifty race, a no-frills (no fee, no aid, no awards, no wimps) 50-mile race along the Pacific Coast of California designed to undo the extravagant eating that goes on during the holiday season. He has since franchised (for no fee) the Fat Ass Fifty to more than three dozen sites in a dozen countries.

His urge for options also came almost simultaneously with his growing interest in competing in triathlons. He competed in the famed Hawaii Ironman Triathlon, he was instrumental in founding *Triathlon* magazine, and he created the Escape From Alcatraz Triathlon, the first leg of which is swimming through the icy waters of San Francisco Bay from Alcatraz to San Francisco.

But Joe's appetites seem never to be sated. Triathlons gradually became too tame. Something a mite more challenging was called for. So Joe, now 62, put together an around the world "trip" in which he would circle the globe in several stages in various forms of basic locomotion. He started in 1990 by bicycling from Alaska to New York. Other legs have included swimming across the international date line from Russia's Big Diomede to Alaska's Little Diomede Island and sailing across the Atlantic. In 1997, Oakes uncorked his next-to-last leg. At the end of the famed Iditarod dogsled race in Alaska, he hooked up with one of the mushers and borrowed a team to go backwards along the trail. His last leg will involve canoeing from Fairbanks to Kaltag on the Yukon River.

In between adventures, Oakes continues to direct the Escape From Alcatraz Triathlon. He also served several terms as president of the Dolphin South End Running Club, running in the footsteps of Walt Stack, one of his heroes.

Advice? One of Oakes' favorite pieces of advice, borrowed from Walt Stack, is "Keep breathing," and from Frank Zappa: "Look out where those huskies go, and do not eat the yellow snow."

Oakes has taken his running to extremes most runners can only dream of. He's run at and competed at every imaginable distance and run in every corner of the world. If there is a lesson to be learned toward keeping one's running fresh, Joe Oakes rates an A+ on the final exam.

Don't Over-Race

The older we become, the more careful we should be about selecting our races. While a younger runner can race literally every weekend and still keep coming back for more, a mature runner needs at least alternate weekends off to help the recuperation process along. While 5K and 10K and even 10-mile races can be a wonderful way to get a speed workout in, overdoing it by racing too often can run the aging body into a pit of injuries out of which it's impossible to climb.

Some of the problem involved here is that although we are constantly aging physically, each of us is stuck mentally at some age that is a fraction of our calendar age. If you still function mentally as though you are 19, the feeling of inde-structibility that comes hard-wired with that age is still at least partially in place, even if it's hanging on by two or three very fragile wires.

We tend, almost, to get into ruts. If at age 35 we raced every weekend from April through October, we tend not to change that habit until something significant comes along to force us to consider changing it, such as a recurring injury.

This goes hand-in-hand with the compulsive nature of some runners. If a runner has a string of 15 Humboldt Redwoods Marathons going, he or she is likely to throw common sense to the wind and go for number 16 even if currently nursing a pesky hamstring problem.

Some runners are strong enough and biomechanically sound enough that they can roll through their 40s and into their 50s before this accumulating overuse catches up to them. Others are not so lucky, and endure recurring injuries on an annual basis because they have never, under the physical dictates of advancing age, modified down their racing schedule.

There is an old saying that goes, "Pick your fights carefully." The same applies to racing.

Always Cool Down After a Run

Seeing runners at the end of a race stop immediately after crossing the finish line and just plop themselves onto a nearby grassy knoll sends shivers down my spine the same way seeing runners stretch themselves into obscene shapes on a chilly morning before a race does.

What a shock that delivers to the body that has just spent the past hour or two performing at a high level. Suddenly, all body systems are turned off. Problem is, they aren't turned off. The runner may have stopped, but the body systems are still going at top speed.

The older the runner, the more profound the body's backlash is likely to be from such an abrupt stop. Such a stop is a good way to shock the heart into confusion over what it is supposed to be doing.

Dr. Kenneth Cooper, in his 1986 book *Running Without Fear*, examines the death of Jim Fixx and lays out some of the body's reactions to the immediate cessation of exercise:

> *By standing motionless, even for a few moments, Jim may have triggered a series of events that culminated in his death. As he came to a halt, about 60 percent of the blood in his body would have begun to 'pool,' or collect, below his waist. This customarily happens after a vigorous run. Simultaneously, the blood would have drained away from his heart and brain, and he would have become light-headed.*
>
> *Then, his heart rate would have fallen rapidly — that's called 'bradycardia,' an abnormally slow heart rate. Jim would have quickly begun to get even more light-headed and nauseous, and before he was aware*

of what was happening, he would have lost con-
sciousness. His blood pressure would also have fallen
and triggered this production of adrenal hormones,
which in such circumstances try to stimulate the heart
to beat faster.

One overreacting response of the body after the other conspired to ultimately kill him.

When finishing up a workout, the best cool-down is simply
to roll into a walk or stroll until your heart gradually brings
itself down under control. A good rule of thumb is to walk
roughly one-third of a mile for every five run. An additional
benefit of this routine is that the walking will help loosen up
the legs and massage away some of the tightness, which leaves
them in better condition for your next day's workout.

Cool-down does not have to be long, drawn-out, or complex.
Walk yourself back to a relaxed heart rate, and give your heart
the courtesy of gently paying it back for the service it just
rendered your running.

chapter

17

Injuring

*"Our greatest glory is not
in never falling, but in
rising every time we fall."*

—Confucius

This chapter is in no way meant as a substitute for professional sports medical attention to your running injuries. Medium to serious running injuries should be treated by professionals specializing in sports medicine, which is a growing field these days. It is also a field that has developed treatment methods that a decade ago would have seemed miracle cures.

Since most running injuries are to the feet, ankles, or legs, the runner's first medical resource is a podiatrist or orthopedic surgeon specializing in sports. Better still, a podiatrist or orthopedic surgeon who runs.

For the older runner, it is also a good idea to be on a first-name basis with an internist from whom you receive a general physical exam each year. Again, it's a plus if your internist is a runner, so he'll be in sync with the fact that some of your vital signs point to an excess of fitness in an unfit world and not necessarily toward some malady.

Nor is this chapter meant as a home remedy manual. There are several excellent medical guides for runners on the market that are written by sports medicine professionals. Much of the information in those guides can help diagnose running injuries or can help the injured runner treat certain injuries common to runners.

This chapter is meant as a short guide toward heading off injuries that may be imminent and for treating extremely minor injuries with an eye toward making certain they don't become more serious. It is also a paean to the healing wonders of rest.

The Difference Between Ache and Pain

The act of running, especially the act of running seriously, can leave the runner with well-earned aches that can and often do last for days. There is absolutely nothing wrong with feeling aches in the wake of a workout. This is a natural process. The body is physically stressed by the running and consequently is not shy at presenting evidence of that stress. Which is why it is important to schedule in several easy days after a particularly long or hard workout: the body needs time to adjust to the new level of stress.

Occasionally runners who lay off working out for several weeks experience aches in certain body parts because they *haven't* been exercised recently. Even sedentary people experience aches in various parts of the body, perhaps more so than runners do, which is ironic, in a sense, since they are usually aches of inertia.

It is important to be able to differentiate between aches (which are a natural consequence of exercise) and pains, which are arrows pointing directly at a body part that is about to be injured or is already injured. An ache is a dull, vague, ongoing, eventually diminishing reminder that a body part has undergone some serious use. A pain is a sharp, either intermittent or continuous, unpleasant sensation that is easy to pinpoint.

It is not uncommon, for instance, to develop a sharp pain at the outside of the knee if your running shoes are worn down at the outside of the heel. The sharp, very-easy-to-pinpoint pain may go away after you stop running. But if the problem with the worn shoe is not corrected, during and after the next run the pain may last longer and be more severe, until a knee injury develops.

Wallow in your aches in the wake of long or hard workouts or races; the ache is a manifestation of the work you've expended in your running. But be very conscious of even the smallest pain. It is often an indicator that something more serious is about to develop at that spot.

DR. GEORGE SHEEHAN

For veterans of the First Running Revolution (1976–80), Dr. George Sheehan holds a very special place in their hearts and minds as the philosopher/guru of the sport.

Considering how much ready scientific knowledge is available today relative to the physical and mental benefits of running, we forget how little was available in 1976. In those days people took up running more on faith than on science.

A handful of medical doctors (Kenneth Cooper, Jack Scaff, Tom Bassler, and George Sheehan) contended that not only was it all right for adults to run long distances, but that it was actually good for them. Based on what? Based on a handful of raw data, their observations, and what Dr. George Sheehan referred to as his "experiment of one." That translated to George making scientific observations on how long-distance running was affecting him, then extrapolating it to the larger population of increasingly sedentary Americans.

George Sheehan was a good runner in his youth. But like so many other Americans who were not encouraged to pursue such a frivolous activity beyond their youth, he gave it up as he became a cardiologist. Ironic, to be sure.

"At the age of 45, I pulled the emergency cord and ran out into the world," George wrote of his conversion to latter-life runner. "It was a decision that meant no less than a new life, a new course, a new destination. I was born again in my 45th year." Not long after, George Sheehan would also birth a writing career.

As luck would have it, just as Dr. Sheehan was being born as a writer in his 50th year, Joe Henderson, who had worked at *Track & Field News,* was taking over as editor of *Runner's World,* which had just changed its name from *Distance Running News* and moved to California. George Sheehan offered to answer some medical questions in issues of the redesigned *Runner's World* and Joe was eager to fire up a new column under his new editorship. The year was 1970 and was the beginning of a partnership that would last more than 25 years.

George began fielding running medical questions from readers of *Runner's World* and answering them. His answers shook up much of the staid medical world. He was an early advocate of consulting a podiatrist if you had a running injury. Some of his solutions to running problems were as much homespun remedies as remedies you'd likely find in medical journals. The popularity of the column exploded.

But George had more to say about running than mere medical answers would allow. Joe gave George a second column: "Dr. Sheehan on Running." It quickly became the most popular column in the magazine. What did "Dr. Sheehan on Running" do? That's a hard one to answer. The short answer is that it assured adult runners that not only was it OK to run, but it was a good— even blessed—thing to do. George Sheehan in 700 words per month extolled the virtues of running and runners and quoted—and sometimes misquoted—every philosopher he could lay his hands on to make his point. The column made average runners feel more relaxed, more assured, more confident, more joy-filled in what they were doing.

"What makes cowards of us all is not conscience as Shakespeare suggested, not fatigue as Vince Lombardi claimed, but pain," George wrote in one of his columns. "Pain and fear of that pain is our undoing. Nowhere is this more evident than in athletics."

Let's face it, it's the rare writer who can get Shakespeare and Vince Lombardi in the same sentence.

George's new column by itself was a touchstone in the burgeoning sport of long-distance running. But the column was nothing if George didn't live his talk and continue his "experiment of one." There can be no doubt but that he did just that. He ran Boston regularly, at the age of 50 he set a world record in the mile in his age group, and at the age of 61 he did the unimaginable.

His beloved Boston Marathon, in part to stem the groundswell of participants, imposed a strict standard: old men must run below 3:10 in order to qualify for the race. George, who had never run below 3:10 in a marathon, was irate. His columns literally sizzled with his ire that older runners, those whom nature had gradually robbed of minutes per year from their potential marathon speed, should be conspired against by the nabobs at Boston.

An irate George Sheehan was a wonder to behold. But an irate George Sheehan was also an inspired George Sheehan. He decided that he'd beat Boston at its own game. Never one to train with what could be termed a strict routine, George took the bit in the mouth and went to work. He would train for a sub-3:00. Later that year, at the Marine Corps Marathon, George Sheehan, 61 years of age, ran a 3:01 marathon!

He'd failed to break the magic 3:00 barrier, but by god, he'd come close. At least he'd tried. In his failure he was ecstatic. The effort to train for a sub-3:00 marathon and the race that came from it rejuvenated him. It had trained him to be a running animal as he'd seldom been before. In failure, his experiment of one had succeeded—beyond his wildest dreams.

As he shared the victory of his failure with his readers, each of his readers gloried in the positive effort that had gone into their own glory-tinted failures. George had once again connected with his fellow runner as no other writer could. He—and they—were once again born again, a process that continues in his beloved fellow runners years after his own death.

Warnings of Injury

Our bodies communicate with us all the time. We're used to and familiar with our body telling us it's sleepy or hungry or thirsty or horny. But it also gives us hints—often numerous hints—that something is amiss or about to go wrong. Heart attacks, for instance, don't usually come out of nowhere. Heart disease is generally a glacial process, with plenty of little hints given off along the way like the sharp cracking sounds a real glacier gives off.

It's much the same with running injuries. Besides the obvious pain that can hint at or herald a running injury, the body can give other indications of potential trouble. Excessive deadness in the legs in the wake of too many miles or miles done too hard can be a warning that they are about to give out at their weakest link if you continue to push them. High resting pulse rate is a certain indication that the body has not recuperated properly and will give out at a weak point if it is pushed farther. Sore or cracking or bleeding nailbeds are a sign of overtraining and a precursor to breakdown.

Listen to the early warning hints your body gives off and quickly head off more serious problems.

Ice and Heat

It is easy to pick out the experienced marathoners back at the host hotel after the race, especially if the hotel has a swimming pool and an adjoining hot tub or spa. The novices are soaking in the hot tub while the veterans are standing waist-deep in the cool water of the pool. The cool water serves to reduce some of the post-race swelling and inflammation in the muscles and joints while the hot water encourages swelling and inflammation.

The rule of thumb for using ice and heat to treat or head off injuries is ice for the first 72 hours, heat thereafter. Although heat can feel good on a sore or painful injury and will encourage blood flow that will carry away injured cells and bring in oxygen and nourishment to the affected area, much of the discomfort at the site of an injury is due to swelling and inflammation, the body's reaction to the injury. By icing the sore area as quickly as possible following an injury or by icing a sore area to prevent it from becoming an injury, the runner does tend to slow the natural healing process. But icing also tends to prevent the soreness or injury from becoming more pronounced and serious if the body part is going to be used again before it is completely healed.

For instance, if you have a sore Achilles tendon (which heals very slowly, due to very limited blood access), you will likely not be able to stay in bed with it for the several days it may take for it to improve. You need to get up and get to work or go to meetings or do chores. If the injury is serious enough or if it gives indications that it could become serious if it is run on again, it is of course best not to run on it, but you may still need to use it in the normal course of a day. Icing the affected part slows and controls the swelling and inflammation and tends to give the part more ease of movement than it would have if the swelling and inflammation is allowed to set in or if it is encouraged to set in by soaking the Achilles in a hot bath.

There are several cautions when it comes to using ice, however:

1. Don't wrap or press the ice directly against the skin or it will tend to burn the skin. Instead, wrap the ice in a towel or washcloth before wrapping an Ace bandage around it to hold it to the affected area.

2. Do not go running on an Achilles tendon or any other body part you've just concluded icing. The area will be somewhat numbed and anesthetized by the cold and will tend to be more inflexible than it would be if it were warm. It is easy to reinjure a part that is iced.

3. Don't keep the ice on the affected part indefinitely. Ice for 15 to 30 minutes, then remove the ice and allow the affected part to come back to room temperature. Reapply the ice several hours later.

As far as the heat side of the equation goes, the application of heat after 72 hours loosens the affected part and tends to move blood to and from the area faster, which tends to speed the healing process. As with the ice, do not apply the heat directly to the area unless the heat is mild and will not burn the skin. And don't leave the heat on too long. Give the affected part time to come back to room temperature for an hour or two before reapplying heat.

The proper application of ice and heat can go a long way toward controlling a running injury, and both come relatively cheap compared to the consequences of ignoring such simple treatment.

The Changing Foot

Although the feet we have at 50+ are essentially the same feet we've had all our lives, they have been altered by time and gravity. Certainly the foot in later life does not undergo the dramatic growth and changes it that in the first 18 years. But there are changes that affect us as runners.

For one thing, 50 years worth of serving as our body's foundation against the pressures of gravity tend to depress the foot's arch—if it had one to start with. The tendons and bands in the foot have stretched and become more slack. These downward trends in the foot have also served to spread it, which can result in the foot expanding by a half size or more.

All of which means we need to pay some attention to our feet and give them whatever assistance we can so they can continue to serve us. Just because we wore a size 9 at age 25 doesn't mean that's the size we need at 65. As we age, our height lessens and our feet spread. Who thought up that plan?

If you have even any minor aches in the feet, it would be worth consulting a podiatrist on a bi-yearly basis. You may need a minor arch support to accommodate a tired and deconstructing arch. You may need a minor heel lift to accommodate too-tight too-long Achilles tendons. Because of your expanding feet, you may need to move up a shoe size to better assure continued good health in your feet.

It is much easier and a whole lot cheaper to spoil your feet by having them checked every two years so that you can incorporate usually simple and inexpensive preventative measures rather than waiting until something gives out.

I compare this to the sorry state many of the country's bridges are in because they were not properly maintained. Good maintenance would have been much less expensive in the long run than the cost of replacing the bridges because they have now deteriorated to the point they are no longer safe or functional. But at least they have one thing going for them that your feet haven't: you can replace the bridge (at great cost), but you're stuck with the feet down there at the end of your legs.

A little attention to your changing and evolving feet can go a long way toward keeping you on the roads and running across the bridges for literally as late into your life as you choose.

Chronic Injuries

You're almost not a runner if you haven't got at least one chronic injury that you can call to mind without a moment's notice. The very nature of running long distances on hard surfaces invites overuse injuries. And few of us are biomechanically perfect enough to avoid them—especially when you consider the miles that pile up over decades of running.

© Beth Schneider

Chronic is a two-headed beast. It refers to both long-standing and recurring injuries: those that won't go away as well as those that won't stay away. Chronic injuries are common to some runners because once a body part is injured, it tends to be weakened and therefore more susceptible to reinjury.

If you've run for any length of time and are burdened with a chronic injury, it is more likely that you are running around it rather than through it. By that I mean that you (and perhaps your sports medicine specialist) have come up with some way of allowing you to continue running in spite of still suffering from the chronic injury. This can involve anything from a podiatrist prescribing orthotics to compensate for a foot injury to a runner who has given up running on asphalt in preference to dirt in response to chronic problems from the former.

Chronic injuries that are not attended to or that are run through are often career-ending injuries, although some of them can be corrected with surgical intervention. Fortunately surgery, especially knee surgery, has taken incredible strides over the past decade, and some running careers that seemed over have been revived. Again, when a chronic injury presents itself, consult the sports medicine specialists.

Chronic injuries that are recurring should also be dealt with by consulting a sports medicine expert. However, a knowledgeable runner who pays attention to his or her body and who keeps a good training log can often get on top of recurring injuries by tracing back what precipitates them and then altering the training to avoid whatever it is that sets them off.

Recurring injuries are an ongoing problem for runners in California, where it is so easy and so tempting to run hard all year long. If you run at the same level all year long, at some point the dreaded Overuse Injury is going to overtake you. And it's fascinating how the very same sequence of events can repeat themselves at the very same time of the year, year after year, producing the same injury.

We need to periodically back down on our mileage and give our bodies a rest so they can heal themselves. If we arrogantly force our bodies through workouts day after day, week after week, something's going to give. It's really that simple.

And curing recurring chronic injuries can be just that simple: track your training backwards from the injury and 9 out of 10 times you'll be able to analyze the problem yourself. And you'll be able to "cure" it yourself by avoiding the syndrome you've created to cause it.

When you pull down the logs to analyze the problem, remove yourself and your emotions from the equation, pretend that the logs you are examining belong to someone else, and play detective. Remove the emotional involvement and you'll be pleasantly surprised at how astute you are in the Science of Overuse—and in formulating a solution.

Again, failing finding a solution yourself, your sports medicine specialist is your prime resource, and well worth the investment of a consultation.

What to Do When an Injury Is Obvious

In a word: Stop! No injury is going to be made better by continuing to use the affected part. Stop immediately. Assess the injury. If it is an obvious injury, don't despair. Obvious injuries, injuries that are easy to diagnose, are injuries that have probably been suffered by literally tens of thousands of runners before, and can and have just as obviously been treated.

Take two days off from running. If the injury is painful or uncomfortable even when you are not running on it, schedule a visit to the appropriate sports medicine specialist. If the injury is painful or uncomfortable only when you put weight on it, get off it, ice it, and give it at least two additional days of rest.

If it vanishes after the first two days off plus the additional two days, try walking three to five miles briskly on it. If there is no recurrence, take another day's rest, and then begin back with a very gentle, two-mile shuffle.

If it continues to show no signs of pain or discomfort, ease back into your running program. Do not, however, jump back into your program at the point at which you dropped out when the potential injury struck. To do so will only aggravate the potential injury. Treat your body gently in easing back into running and pay special attention to the spot that appeared to act up on you.

If, under more ambitious training, it begins to give off hints it is still not right, consult a sports medicine specialist. Don't attempt to run through the discomfort. It's only common sense that to do so carries with it the potential to do real damage. You've only got one body, and although it is possible to have some parts replaced, the replacement parts are not as good as the original equipment. Treat your running body with respect and tenderness. It got you this far; it deserves to be babied when you run it into trouble.

Follow this rule with your running in order to extend it as far as possible into your dotage: when in doubt, don't.

What Not to Do When an Injury Is Obvious

When an injury makes itself known and is obvious to you, don't run on it. Give it a rest. Analyze the nature of the injury. Consult a sports medicine specialist if it persists. And then, take the sports medicine specialist's advice.

Don't go to a sports medicine specialist, have your injury analyzed, receive advice from the professional, and then ignore it because you feel the urge to run. Only younger, more rash, less wise runners make mistakes like that. By making mistakes like that, younger runners guarantee that they never get to become older runners.

Do not come back from an obvious injury too soon. Better to come back too slowly, where there are no negative consequences, than to push yourself back too soon, where there is a double-feature of nightmare consequences, nearly all of them bad.

Do not treat your one body with arrogance when it will not perform at a level you want it to when it is incapable of doing so. Trust me on this: you'll never beat your body. It holds all the aces.

Recovering

*"There is no right way
to do something wrong."*

—Unknown

An injured runner is not a pretty sight. Deprived of his or her physical and psychological outlet, the injured runner is often testy, impatient, and typically angry at every other person on the planet who can still run.

There is an addictive quality to running regularly. It is primarily a positive addiction, to be sure: a force that makes it not only possible to keep running, but enjoyable to do so. But deprived of that running fix, the runner begins to exhibit all the symptoms of a classic addict: nervousness, fidgeting, difficulty in concentrating. Apply this to someone in his or her 50s or 60s who's been running 20–30 years and the phenomenon escalates.

And, like the addict, the runner has a very dangerous tendency to cheat—to sneak in some running even though the injury that is preventing running has not healed. It is this nearly uncontrollable urge to come back to running too early from an injury that accounts for so many running injuries turning to chronic—often run-ending—injuries.

In the same way that advice to "When in doubt, do less" works, so does the simple advice to "Take time to heal well." This is especially sound advice for older runners because although most human beings are reluctant to cooperate with the aging process, the aging process goes merrily along working on us whether we want it to or not. Aging first of all opens us to more injuries and second does not allow us to heal as quickly as we have been used to healing.

Path to Recovery

The subject of recovering from a running injury can be covered by what amount to the Five Commandments of Running Injury Recovery:

• *When injured, don't further aggravate the injury by running on it.* There was at one time a macho approach to running injuries that involved "running through an injury." That approach, of course, was not well grounded in the real world, since the inevitable outcome was to further compound the injury. In essence, the runner took an injury and made it much worse than it needed to be. Which meant that it either took even longer to heal or became permanent.

The best way to recover from an injury is to stop doing to the injured part that which injured it. This all sounds boneheadedly simple, and it is, but when caught up in the passion of one's running, common sense is sometimes left locked away in the closet. Even some old, usually wise dogs are susceptible.

The same way that a scab continuously picked at never heals, so too with a running injury. The injury is usually caused by overuse; if you continue to run on it, the overuse turns to self-abuse, and the runner begins to gamble with the possibility of turning a run-of-the-mill injury that would heal on its own into a serious injury that might never heal.

The human body is a wonderfully adaptive organism and, given the correct environment, will often heal itself. The correct environment is rest.

• *Allow 50 percent more time than anticipated for an injury to heal.* This is a rule of thumb that becomes more practical the older we get. A physical action we could accomplish with great

© Ken Lee

finesse at age 25 might take some concentration and work at age 60. That doesn't mean that the task doesn't get done, only that it typically takes a little longer—and is subsequently sometimes done better. This applies to recovering from injuries. If you've paid attention to your body, you'll notice that a flesh wound takes much longer to heal when you're 60 than it did when you were 25. This process of slowing down is natural and inevitable and is so glacial that we usually don't notice it happening—we only notice it once it's happened.

The healing process goes on, but takes its own good time getting there. When dealing with a running injury, it is much better to give it a week more than it needs to heal than a week less. A week less shortchanges the process, while a week more than it needs contributes to its success.

Age + Wisdom = Patience

The best way to turn a transient running injury into a chronic injury is to attempt to come back too early. Take the long view of your running and of your recovery.

• *Find an alternative outlet for your energies.* Besides the fact that running well and regularly becomes a positive addiction and makes us frantic to get back to our running when injured, the process of running builds strength and endurance and when we stop, our energy stores fill up just as they do when we taper for an important race. This sudden buildup of energy contributes to an injured runner being assaulted by the urge to get out and get in a run, no matter how illogical it may be when considering the fact we're supposed to be resting and healing. This sudden energy assault needs an outlet before it becomes self-destructive.

Runners resist substituting nonimpact aerobic exercising while the injured body part heals. Some runners resist alternative exercise just on general principles, sometimes out of pure pigheadedness or cussedness. Others resist it because they feel it is a sort of betrayal of their dedication to running. Others refuse to substitute another activity because very few alternatives are as simple and easy to work into a day as running is.

Having experienced an average share of running injuries and being a bit pigheaded myself, I can speak from experience that although other forms of exercise might not translate perfectly to what you would rather be doing, they are viable alternatives. They have saved many a running career and allowed many a runner to make it safely into the fifth, sixth, even seventh decades still running well.

Bicycle-riding has on numerous occasions served as a viable alternative to pounding out more miles on an injured calf. And running in a pool wearing an aqua-belt has served as an alternative to running six days a week when I was not injured but wanted to prevent injuries when I increased my mileage. Pool workouts are especially good on very hot days during the summer when running would normally be uncomfortable. You'll recall that Joan Benoit Samuelson ran in a pool for weeks as she recovered from surgery before going on to win the gold medal in the 1984 Los Angeles Olympic marathon. Helen Klein has done the same thing to extend her running career. If it's good enough for Helen Klein and Joan Benoit, it should be good enough for us.

There are also, of course, quite a few nonimpact gym-type alternatives to running, including stair-climbing machines, exercise cycles, and rowing machines.

Before frustrating yourself by "suffering" through a running injury, give an alternative exercise a try. After all, the alternative exercise is only temporary, and if it gets you back into your regular running safer and faster, why not make use of it?

• *Follow sound medical advice — to the letter.* It must at times be frustrating to be a sports medicine specialist. I've often felt great masses of compassion for what constitutes a runner's first defensive team against career-shortening injuries because, although an injured runner will go to a sports medicine specialist for treatment and advice, that same runner will very often turn around and completely ignore advice they just paid good money to have a highly-trained expert provide for them. Over the years I've seen runners with stress fractures that require six weeks to heal turn around a week after being put into a cast by an orthopedic surgeon, cut the cast off, and go running. And then blame the surgeon for the fact that the fracture is getting worse, not better.

Sports medicine specialists serve as the runner's first line of defense against becoming injured, and, once injured, the first line of offense toward recovery. If you are injured and take the time to consult with a sports medicine specialist, listen carefully to his or her advice and follow that advice precisely. Period.

• *Never attempt to reenter running at the level you were at when you became injured.* One of the most consistent ways to turn a running injury into a chronic injury is to reenter your training at the level you were when you backed off because of becoming injured. This is so easy to do, since the last memories we have of running are still so vivid that they form an anchor from which we reference our running. It is only natural to want to pick up where we left off. But it can also be very destructive to a running program.

It Takes Time

When coming back from an injury, it is best to take the long view. Ease back into your running program, even if that involves walking or a mixture of walking and running. Not just the injured body part needs and wants this gentling back into training, but all of the other body parts that have been forced to take some time off demand it.

If the injury was mild and of short duration, a week or so, backtrack on your training schedule and ease in at the point you were at three to four months before the injury occurred. If the injury has kept you from running for 10 days or more, treat your comeback almost as though you were starting a running program from scratch—then monitor how your body responds.

It will likely come around with a refreshing vigor, but don't force it to do too much too soon. Many injuries manifest themselves a week or two after they actually occur. Baby yourself as you return to your running. You can always increase the volume and intensity of your workouts if you are undertraining, but you can't back off fast enough to avoid reinjuring yourself if you've come out of the box too quickly.

Give yourself time. After all, what have you got to lose but another injury? And remember this: some of the world's best running performances came in the wake of forced layoffs when world-class runners (Derek Clayton and Joan Benoit come to mind) eased back into their workouts with a fresh resolve to run as well as possible while avoiding reinjuring themselves.

Gard Leighton, a 60+ ultrarunner who owns 10 Western States Trail 100 silver belt buckles, came back off a leg injury to win that 10th buckle. "Sometimes we run so much we forget how good it can be for us to stop occasionally," he said. During his layoff, he did some gentle backpacking. Of course, Gard's "gentle" backpacking would exhaust most llamas.

Injuring yourself is easy; recovering from a running injury is hard, but well worth the effort.

Crashing
(a.k.a. Burnout)

*"The successful man will
profit from his mistakes
and try again in a
different way."*

—Dale Carnegie

It requires no advanced degrees to theorize that when someone does something too long or too much, they can experience burnout. Burnout is different than boredom. We can often work our way through boredom because we can see an end to the boredom if we just look beyond it. With burnout, there is no perceived end in sight. It just is.

Burnout is not uncommon among runners and is usually the result of one of two extremes:

1. The runner feels compelled to run too similarly too often so that boredom turns to burnout.

2. The runner runs so much that running ultimately becomes drudgery.

The first example is typically associated with running used as a prophylactic against heart disease or as a tool for fitness. In this case, the runner is not psychologically wedded to the running, is not passionate about it. It is also usually associated with relatively low mileage, for example, two miles four times a week. This runner never runs far or long enough for the enjoyment of running to take hold because he or she never runs long enough for it to become comfortable. Just as the runner approaches the 40 minutes it takes for the muscles to warm and the second wind to kick in, he stops.

For this type of running burnout, the solution is incredibly simple: increase mileage on alternate days, vary courses, run with friends, and schedule in a race once a month or so. Move running beyond the status of a medicine you take for your health.

It is the second example that is more difficult to deal with: the runner who has essentially run him- or herself out of love with the sport and lifestyle. It is this second example that is our concern here, especially because this is more likely to affect the runner who has many years of running under the waistband of his or her running shorts.

Burnout can come from too much mileage over too long a time, too many races, or too much of both. It can also come in the wake of a supreme running or racing effort, whether the outcome resulted in success or failure.

Spiritual Burnout

Certainly, it is possible to burn out physically. But physical burnout is not our concern here; in most instances, physical burnout can be overcome by a good dose of rest. The burnout that concerns us is more a psychological and/or spiritual overuse injury. I include the term "spiritual" here because some running, especially extreme running or racing, taps into the spiritual well or reservoir and tapped too often or too long, the spiritual well is emptied and takes a tremendous amount of time to refill.

The physical, psychological, and spiritual well concept of running is essential to the sport, and is wonderfully explained by ultramarathon star Ron Kovacs, who holds the 45–49 U.S. age-group records in the 100 miles, 200K, and 24 hours and a 50–54 age-group record in the 100K. Kovacs considers the physical side the least important. As Joe Oakes explains

Kovacs' approach in an article on working walking into your running in the first issue of *Marathon & Beyond* magazine,

The body is merely the physical, the visible, the muscles and bones and blood; it is through this physical entity that Ron propels himself through those endless training and racing miles. He plays with his body, teaches it to love to play. He plays with glycogen, oxygen, food, and time . . . but when, at some point, that physical creature goes into the complaint mode, he switches over to the second well, the mind.

It is this mental side, says Kovacs, that controls, cajoles, and masters the flagging and whining body, pushes it beyond the fun part, into exhaustion and past the plea of 'Please stop, I've had enough!

Eventually, on a tough ultra there comes a time when the mind, too, begins to shred. It is then time to call upon the third and deepest well of all, the spirit. It is from the depths of this spiritual realm that the void of the depleted physical and mental reservoirs can draw up its last source of sustenance. But, says Kovacs, you cannot go to that well too often, because refilling the deep spiritual reservoir is a long, slow process.

RON KOVACS

To say that Ron Kovacs is precise is like saying gravity exists. Trained as an electrical engineer at the University of California/Berkeley in the early 1960s and a 30-year manager at National Semiconductor in the heart of Silicon Valley, Ron is one of ultramarathoning's stalwarts as well as one of the sport's most astute students—and one of its most consistent practitioners.

Fifty-nine years old on October 22, 1997, Ron has salted away age-group ultra long-distance records for decades.

On February 12, 1994 at the 100K (62 miles) USATF championships held in Sacramento, California, Ron set a 55–59 age-group record of 9 hours and 21 minutes and 53 seconds. On January 1–2, 1993, he broke an age-group record for a 48-hour track run by 13 miles when he completed 202 miles and placed second overall; unfortunately, first place (213 miles) was taken by another runner in his age-group, who won the race outright.

Married to his high school sweetheart and the grandfather of three, Ron brings the scientist's approach to longer distance running by studying the distance to be run and then by training precisely for that challenge. He doesn't claim to be the most talented runner, but he is almost always the most knowledgeable and best-prepared.

A veteran of the Hawaii Ironman, Ron has also earned a silver buckle at the Western States 100 Trail Run on five occasions for completing the grueling course in under 24 hours—all after the age of 40.

Ron is one of the pioneers of carefully working walking into running in order to compete more effectively at ultra distances. It has not been uncommon for Ron to go to work on Friday, come home and do a 60-mile night workout beginning at 8:00 P.M. and ending at 8:00 A.M., shower, catch a few hours sleep, breakfast, and take care of the yardwork. The night workouts are important for approaching 100-mile races, where the competitor is guaranteed that a fair amount of the race will be done throughout the night.

Ron is an advocate of incorporating some classic designs into his extra-long workouts. His overnight workouts are typically set up in a pyramid format, where he runs 25 minutes and walks 5, then runs 20 and walks 5, then runs

15 and walks 5, then runs 10 and walks 5, then runs 5 and walks 5, then runs 10 and walks 5, then runs 15 and walks 5, then runs 20 and walks 5, and finally runs 25 and walks 5.

While taking a scientific approach to his sport, Ron is also a student of its history, on which he bases his run/walk approach. He has studied the incredible feats of the 19th-century pedestrians as well as feats of more modern adventure runners who have run/walked solo across the United States.

Ron is also a philosopher of the sport of ultrarunning. He is a firm believer that there are three levels of ultra-distance running: the physical, the psychological, and the spiritual. The physical is, to Ron, the least important of the three, while the spiritual is the most deep-seated and least likely to be quickly renewed if tapped too deeply too often.

"You cannot go to that well [the spiritual well] too often," Ron says, "because refilling the deep spiritual reservoir is a long, slow process."

Ron also feels there is no ultimate age at which one needs to give up running/walking. "The more you do, the more you can," Ron feels. His records prove him correct.

Two Types of Burnout

There are essentially two types of burnout a runner faces, one of a very specific nature, the other more complex and wide-ranging.

Think of the first type of burnout as Single-Barreled Burnout. This is burnout centered on your running, and the one on which we'll spend most of this chapter. It is burnout due to too much running too long or at too intense a level.

The second type of burnout is referred to as Double-Barreled Burnout and is a burnout in your running that is not due solely to running. It is when your running is negatively affected by your experiencing overload in several other areas of your life. This can be a running burnout brought about by anything from job loss before retirement to one of the kids moving back home—along with the three grandchildren. It is a confluence of too many stressful or overwhelming events that knock the underpinnings from your running, causing your running to become just one more stressor in your life.

Single-Barreled Burnout

There are three progressive stages runners go through when facing single-barreled burnout: their runs become stale, good runs happen less often, and finally they stop running altogether.

Staleness: The Early Warning System

Long before a runner burns out on the process of running, there are warnings, the most common of which is staleness.

Staleness is usually a feeling of merely going through the motions of running as though they are an obligation instead of a joy. Staleness can be physical or psychological—or both.

Physically, running too long at too high a level can bring on staleness. This often accompanies an attempt to hold a peak or at least a hill for way too many months and usually occurs when a runner is negatively addicted or the runner lives in a geographic area where the difference between the seasons is so minimal that it is possible to run easily all year long. In the latter instance, it is especially tempting to tempt fate by drawing out a running season that has gone especially well. Unfortunately, like nature itself, the runner needs times of growth and other periods of relative idleness before the next growth spurt. This tends to affect older rather than younger runners simply because the older runner has had the opportunity to run many more miles over many more years.

The staleness can be either physical or mental or both. It is a deadness in the running. Every one of us has the occasional day when we walk out the door to do a run and, for whatever reason (often too many other stressors on our mind), we ask ourselves, "What the hell am I doing?" On those occasions, some of us give in to the question, turn around, walk back into the house, and don't do the run; or we cut the run short rather than having to fight against the seeming inertia.

If that kind of a day hits once every month or two, there is little cause for concern. Again, those days can be brought on by an especially long season or while building mileage or intensity for a specific effort. The stride toward burnout comes when the staleness seems to have invaded your running program and it becomes the rare instance when you walk out the door to go on a run and actually find it uplifting.

What can you do about staleness so that it doesn't escalate to burnout? At a younger age, the advice would probably be to see if you can run through it. Beyond 50 years of age, however, pushing through the staleness may not raise you to the next plateau of strength and discipline, but may very well break down both you and your program.

The first step against the staleness is to give yourself a break. Declare an end to your running season, cut back on the intensity, take an extra day's rest each week, and give your running a change of scenery. It may be worth the drive of several miles to place your run into a more pleasant, less predictable scene than you've been using. Is there a course you haven't run in six months? Run it, but run it slowly and take in the scenery. Place your run into a different context. Can you work a run into a weekend picnic or into a trip to a change of scenery where you are exploring new territory?

Often a good way to get out from under the staleness is to sit down with a calendar and plan out your next six months of running, but with a radically different focus. If you've been a marathoner, consider changing your prime focus for the next year to going for a fast time in the mile. Long term, the change in emphasis often benefits your normal focus. The work to increase your leg speed so that you can do a mile well will certainly translate to giving you better leg speed when you again take up the marathon.

Staleness can often be moderated by revising your usual courses. Do you run your courses in the same direction? Run them backwards. Hook several of your normal courses together and make different courses. It is so easy to fall into the rut of doing the same courses over and over to the point that they become a detriment to your running program.

Consider also changing the time of day you run, even if it is for only one day a week. You may not have found your true running niche in the day. Just because you've been running first thing in the morning doesn't necessarily mean it is the only time of the day when you can run and enjoy it. Studies indicate that an athlete performs best in the mid- to late-afternoon.

Brownout

This is the stage between staleness and burnout. You feel as though you've burned out but still occasionally have a wonderful run—to the point that it sparkles like a diamond among coal. Keep on the same track, however, and the brownout turns to burnout when the diamonds become too scarce to remember.

When staleness or brownout occurs, the first two lines of defense are to take an extra day of rest and to cut back on the intensity and volume of workouts. Take the running (and racing) out of the context of stressor, haul it back in as outlet or entertainment or hobby.

Under brownout conditions, if you are racing cut your racing in half with an eye toward bringing your season to an early end. This is something that Uta Pippig's coach has done consistently to keep her running and racing fresh, and it has obviously worked.

On weekday workouts, leave the watch at home. Just go out and run through the course. Take in the scenery as you go. Occasionally wander, throwing in a back road or a street you don't normally run, even if it changes your workout by a half-mile one way or the other.

And here's one of the most difficult suggestions for a runner who tends toward the hard-core: change one or two of the workouts per week to either bicycling or swimming. Runners don't like to engage in other aerobic sports at first, but the other sport can grow on you much as the running did. For those of us over 50, using bicycling or swimming at least two times a week changes the workout context, but also will improve the remaining runs because both bicycling and swimming get the runner off legs that may be feeling a season's worth of serious running—and tiredness in the legs can be a big contributor to staleness and brownout. You command the legs to do what they did willingly three months ago, and they don't, and it can distress the runner right into a mental brownout. This tendency toward staleness becomes more common, of course, the longer you've been running, so older runners with lots of miles on their legs and heads are much more susceptible to this tendency than are relatively new runners.

As with staleness, consider putting the kabosh on brownout by changing the focus of your running. If you've been running only roads, add trails one or two times a week. Trail running requires developing a whole new set of skills and besides, trail running will provide a much more impact-friendly surface on which to run. Your legs will thank you for it. Running trails also takes the runner back to the basics of running. Long before there was macadam, there were dirt trails. Consider putting together an autumn cross-country season on the way to winding down for the off-season. The softer surface will help your legs recover from a long season of road training and racing, and the change of scenery and the art of leaping over rocks and roots will change your mental focus and lighten up the brownout. The eye–leg coordination is also a terrific mental exercise for older runners that keeps the mind sharp and that translates to better, smoother running and movement in general. Make certain to stick with the plan to wind down into an off-season, though. Just because the cross-country running makes you feel better about your running and about yourself, you made a deal with your head and your legs to give them some well-deserved time off. Follow up on your promise.

Burnout

If you've ever been burned to the ground in your running, you know what's involved. You have to literally have someone else push you out the door to run, and when you do run, it's nearly always too much like work. There are no diamonds on the runs. None. Only coal and rust.

Burnout is literally overuse of the mind, often aggravated by a body that's been run into the ground. This sad state requires radical surgery, or it promises to end your running life as you knew it.

Allow me to digress to a personal story that illustrates this condition. After 12 years of running and enjoying it, 35 marathons, a half-dozen ultras, and a handful of tough but memorable track races, running friend Tom Crawford and I decided to become the first runners in history to run from Badwater in Death Valley (at 282 feet, lowest point in the Western Hemisphere and hottest and driest spot on Earth) to the peak of Mt. Whitney (at 14,494 feet, highest point in the contiguous U.S.) and back, a distance of just under 300 miles. We planned to do this in mid-summer. No one had ever even considered trying the out-and-back course. Tom had been the fifth person in history to run from Badwater to Whitney's peak (1986) and ran it again in 1987 as part of a U.S. versus U.K. race. I'd never run the course; I traditionally ran badly in heat and consistently suffered altitude sickness at heights well below 14,000 feet. But we made a pact to do it.

My goal was to break seven days. In July of 1989 we successfully did the course. But I fell nearly three hours short of my goal. Being goal-oriented, I returned to the course in 1991 and with 274 miles down, dropped when it seemed as though I might have developed a stress fracture in my lower leg; it turned out to be ligamentitis.

I jumped right back into training and returned to Death Valley in July of 1992—to some of the most consistently hot weather they'd enjoyed in years. I finally broke seven days, but in the process was forced to pretty well drain the spiritual well, while also messing up my Achilles tendons.

For two years I nursed my Achilles tendons back to health by conservative shoe insert experiments, but I was in no hurry for anything much to happen because my joy of running had been seared away. If I ran at all, it was three times a week, and sometimes it was difficult to get out the door to run three miles.

Running had become more of a haunting nuisance than a joy. Occasionally I'd have a run that felt halfway decent and that hinted at what now seemed like fading memories of running well. But each time I picked up the pace or added miles, I could feel the spiritual well being drained anew.

After one particularly distressing hobble through a 5K workout (and "workout" is the correct word), I sat down at the picnic table in the backyard and questioned where I was going with my running. I realized I was on the edge. Push too hard and my running was past. Or else give it all the time it needed to come back. Note, not all the time *I* needed, but all the time *it* needed. I decided to run at *its* speed, not dictate *my* desires onto it.

There were some basic facts I needed to deal with:

- It was going to be a long road back healing my Achilles tendons and I'd best become comfortable with wearing running shoe inserts for the rest of my life.
- My previous aversion to running in the heat had multiplied its power due to the searing week running in Death Valley. Running in any kind of heat would require dipping, yet again, into the spiritual well, which would in turn keep the well drained.
- Until the spiritual well refilled, my running would hold little joy.

I admit along the road back I made some mistakes, most often brought on by enthusiasm for a short run that went well and that I pushed a bit too hard, thereby once again dipping into the far-from-filled spiritual well. I compared notes with other long-term runners and constantly reexamined within myself the reasons for running, realizing that it didn't owe me, I owed it.

From examining the experience of burnout as it progressed and by consulting with runners I respect, among them Jeff Galloway and Joe Henderson, two things became crystal clear. The first was to translate the delayed gratification distance runners hone so well into a cloud of patience from which I would watch the spiritual well refill. And the second thing was that there are some rather . . .

Radical Steps You Can Take

Here are four direct ways to eliminate burnout:

• Stop running. Ah, the heresy. Seriously, just plain stop running. Become a nonrunner. Hide running shoes way in the back of closets. Put race T-shirts in cardboard boxes and put them in the garage. Withdraw somewhat from the running scene, which wasn't all that difficult for me since I'm more of a solitary runner anyway. Become a watcher rather than a doer. To stay attached to running, if even tenuously, volunteer more often to help at races but do not, under any circumstances, race. Do some of the things there was no time to do because training and racing took so much time and dedication. Be patient. Add a few pounds. Become as good at being a nonrunner as you'd been at being a runner. It takes practice, but heck, millions of people are very good at not running. If they could not do it, I could not do it.

• At some point into the nonrunner mode there would be a day when the leaves would begin to turn, the sun would reach a different angle in the sky, the breeze would have a hint of winter, and the mind would return to cross-country running in college. And there would be the urge to go out for a run. Don't. Instead, go to the calendar, note the date, turn the page and mark the same date in the next month as the date you will "restart" your running program as a novice, from the ground up.

• In the interim, read *Loneliness of the Long Distance Runner*, not because it is about running, which it isn't, but because it is about something else: it is about the rest of life, and about priorities. It helps place running in perspective to that larger sum.

• Restart running at a novice, first-timer, entry-level stage: very conservatively, three to four times a week, two to three miles at a time, no speed, few hills; keep it basic, the way it was when you started. This allows you to retake control of your running. If, at any point, the running feels as though it is a strain, as though it is demanding more of you than you are comfortable giving at that point, stop and walk home. The psychological and especially the spiritual wells need plenty of time to refill. Allow them that time. Allow yourself that flexibility.

On the plus side, because you have a history of running, your return to running will come faster and easier than it did when you first began. Even on a molecular level, the memory of how to run is hard-wired, and during the process of restarting, the ability to run well tends to come back fairly fast. The challenge is to control the rate at which it comes back so that you stay on top of it.

During this process of returning, it is one of the only times it would be appropriate to run farther—or faster—than planned on occasion when the urge strikes. This is a good way to gauge how quickly and well the psychological and spiritual wells are refilling.

During the resurrection of your running, don't schedule too much running too soon and don't overrace.

Double-Barreled Burnout

This is a more painful type of burnout to get through because it isn't the fault of running, it's the fault of everything else.

Each of us has a limit of how much we can do in life and still stay sane. At one end of the spectrum, some people manage quite nicely to become experts at doing virtually nothing. At the other extreme, we have the Martha Stewart Syndrome: the challenge to do as much as we can before we reach our deathbed.

Although it's not unanimous, a fair number of runners are doers: they seem to have a number of projects going on in their lives at the same time. Work. Family. Hobbies. Always pushing, accomplishing. This is especially true of mature runners. Running is important to them, very important, but running also serves as a free shrink: it is a stress release valve; a run is an hour of psychologically coming to grips with the rest of life, it is a time to problem-solve as the distractions camouflaging the real problem fall away.

Unfortunately, people who are this ambitious, this energetic, this consumed with doing things, tend to overcommit themselves, and that overcommitment sometimes catches up to them and becomes a real source of strain if not downright terror. They feel compelled to stand by all commitments, to do it all no matter what the cost to themselves. This is very noble and admirable—to a point. But it isn't worth literally destroying yourself. Life is short enough as it is.

When you find yourself painted into a corner by your own best intentions, allow your running to slide. Again, this sounds like heresy, and to some it is, but if you use your running as your safety valve, and cutting back on its volume or intensity allows you to feel the pressure lift and allows you to fulfill your other commitments, running remains a constant positive force in your life. The last thing you need is to have running become one more stressor.

Keep your running positive by using it to complement the rest of your life. Don't burn out on running because it became an additional stressor, which then changed your perception of it to a negative.

See the next chapter for the best kind of running there is.

*"All of the significant battles
are waged within the self."*

—Sheldon Kopp

Running is just about the cheapest, simplest activity in existence. A good pair of shoes, a pair of running shorts, an old T-shirt, step out the front door, and you're ready to roll.

But isn't it curious that we restless human beings feel obliged to complicate whatever we get our hands on? It's apparently in the genes. We just can't leave well enough alone. For most of us, running has become something much more complex than stepping out the door and heading off at a shuffle.

We tend to imbue running with all sorts of portents and powers, until year after year the baggage our running carries builds up and weighs it down so that instead of becoming something more important and more complex, it merely becomes compromised and even burdensome, injuring us if we do it too much, instilling feelings of guilt if we do it too little.

This is not to say that the act and art of running are not composed of benefits and pitfalls much more complex than the simple act itself. But those benefits and pitfalls come not from the act of running but through our use or misuse of running.

People taken with running have claimed it is everything from a new religion to the solution to all problems while those who've misused it call it every name in the book, and sometimes invent names that aren't in the dictionary, in the process imbuing it with the tremendous power to ruin their lives.

Certainly there are many benefits and pitfalls to running; it is so simple and malleable an activity that it is ready and willing to be fashioned into whatever we will make of it. Unfortunately, bestowing so much power on such a simple act weakens us by compromising our own responsibilities in the process.

© Terry Wild Studio

Running has become so much a part of life for some that they barely think of it at all; they don't have to because it is so integrated into their daily existence. Others pathologically obsess about their running.

When one's running reaches that level of power over a runner's life, it is a good idea to take some time off to quietly sit back and contemplate the role running has played in your life, to review where your running has taken you over the past 5 or 10 years—and to strive to free your running of unnecessary baggage you've saddled it with so that it once again becomes fit, sleek, streamlined, spartan enough to sustain the physical side of your life for the next 5 or 10 years, to head it off from becoming a burden rather than a boon.

What running goals did you set over the past year? Which did you reach? Which did you fail to reach and why? What are some logical but challenging running goals for the next 5 years or 10 years? What have you learned about your running in the past five years that improved your running? Did you learn anything positive from your mistakes? What have you learned about yourself through your running over the past five years? How much of what you've learned about yourself actually came from running and how much of it came from your own basic evolution as a human being?

Take a rainy afternoon off and write an essay of your last year, 5 years, 10 years of running—an essay you'll share with no one, a private review of your running life, a review that separates your running accomplishments from your life. Then put your essay into an envelope and store it somewhere where it will be safe for the next 5 or 10 years, when you can add your next installment.

Then go for a run. A very slow and easy run.

PART

VI

Head Games

Reverting

*"Failure is the opportunity
to begin again
more intelligently."*

—Henry Ford

It is impossible to literally recapture youth. It is not impossible, however, to recapture it figuratively. Fortunately for runners, especially older runners, it is literally *and* figuratively possible to retrieve the early days of your running. And periodically, especially when your running has accumulated too much baggage and complications along the way, it is advisable to do just that: jettison the excess baggage and go back to your running roots for a refreshing revivification.

As we touched upon in the last chapter, an activity as profoundly simple as running is open to being turned into a decidedly complex millstone in a person's life if that person allows it to or places too much emphasis or responsibility on it. Human beings have not only a means and method of doing this, but an almost inbred tendency to do it. We tend to want and need to complicate things in our lives instead of simplifying them. Instead of simply enjoying a beautiful sunset, we haul thousands of dollars' worth of photographic equipment to the seashore and attempt to capture something that can never really be captured. The resulting photo, even a photo taken by the most talented, is a mere approximation of the actual sunset. Where was the gentle ocean breeze that accompanied it? How about the subtle changes the sunset underwent on an almost second-by-second basis? Where is the accompanying sound of the waves crashing the shore?

We tend to do the same thing with relationships, with our personal nostalgia, with our assessment of the power and influence of government, with the enjoyment of a bottle of wine. Everything, to us, must be more than it is in order to justify its—and our—existence.

Running: More or Less

Running, one of the most primordial activities a human being can perform after eating, excreting, sleeping, procreating, and walking around, becomes something much more than it is because we expect so much of it and use it to reflect ourselves off it, yet hold it responsible for our happiness.

Yet occasionally we human beings push through the almost absurd and obscene complications we place upon everything, and break through to the simply profound. We stand there with our jaws drooping and a palm smacked against our forehead, because it is all so very simple. Occasionally, when we forget to place inordinate pressure on our running, we break through to the simple, nearly animal act of doing it, and it is good.

That's why those who are fortunate enough to venture into cross-country running find a special texture and absence of complications in their running. It is why an ultrarunner, once exposed to running trails, never wants to return to asphalt roads.

Although on one level, we are our run because we do it and are it while it is happening (much like W.B. Yeats' contention that "You cannot separate the dancer from the dance . . ."), on most other levels and most other times of the day we are not our run. We are hopefully much more than that, although runners who allow themselves to be sucked into the swamp of obsession literally become no more than their last run, the same way an alcoholic becomes his or her last drink and the cyberslave becomes his or her last poke at the ENTER key.

When we sink to the level of obsessing about our running, we are misusing running as a crutch. And a crutch is an obvious indication that we are damaged. Naturally, being the slave of our running, we feel justified in blaming running for our weakness, our obsession. It is not our fault we are running injured; it is running's fault. We are helpless pawns.

When It's Tougher to Not Do

The strength at that point doesn't involve going out the door for the next run. That's easy. Strength must be applied to not go out the door, to pull back, to stop, to place running in its purest context, to separate *it* from *our* ego.

Take an hour and go to the local park and watch young children playing. They tend to wallow in their animal nature, sprinting from one location to the other, oblivious of all else save the next bit of excitement. They don't obsess about their running. They just do it—without thinking about it.

When our running has accumulated so much excess baggage that it is weighing us down with its heaviosity, it is time to revert to childhood running. Chuck all the trappings. Take a reviving break from running for a month. Read the books you've been meaning to read for years. Check in with your friends again. Stuff the fancy running gear and all the silly accoutrements (including the Walkman if you use one) into a box and stuff the box into the back of a closet.

Keep two pairs of running shorts, two or three pairs of running shoes (preferably one pair that is designated for mud running), and a handful of ratty T-shirts (if possible, none that commemorate races you've run). Throw your chronograph into the box, too.

Shift yourself into neutral as far as your running goes. And open yourself to some radical changes by allowing it to be itself, to be . . . simple.

Reinventing

"Image creates desire.
You will what you imagine."

—J.G. Gallimore

It is the rare person who, distracted by an onslaught of responsibilities and challenges, doesn't allow routine and day-to-day activities to slip into a rut. Running, done long enough and often enough, becomes routine, and can slip into a rut so slowly but inexorably that we don't even notice. The sides of the rut are gentle but slick.

We've discussed before the woman who ran the same 10-mile course every day. If she was using her run as a daily meditation and escape from the rest of her life, she certainly found her route to success; but if she was running for the love of running, although her course was a loop, she was running down a blind alley.

There are two angles from which to reinvent (and thereby invigorate) running. The first is to come at it anew, as discussed in the previous chapter: bring your burdened running program to a grinding halt, take a break from it (and it from you), cast off its mundanities, then restart as though you are new to the sport. The second method is to take a very hard look at your running program, then make major modifications in order to reinvent it.

There is a multitude of ways to modify and reinvent a running program. We'll examine five methods. Some of the methods will seem nearly too obvious to mention, yet for many runners who have slipped into ruts, the obvious is too often obscured.

Change the Time of Day You Run

Scientists have determined that the maximal time of day for athletic performance is in the late afternoon. Some of the world's best marathon performances have occurred after the clock passed noon.

Yet scientists also know that human beings are hard-wired before birth with a tendency to be either a lark or an owl: someone who functions well as an early bird as opposed to someone whose body and spirit begin to rev up as the sun goes down. I spent three years in college with a roommate who was an owl to my lark. It was quite an experience. When I came back from 10 o'clock classes, he was still sleeping, yet he'd cap off his late-night studying in the lounge with a late, late night movie on the old black and white TV.

As far as our running goes, most of us have made arrangements to fit it into a specific portion of our day and, once it is so placed, it stays there. We get up early and run before the rest of the day begins or we use our lunch hour to run or we run in the late afternoon. We tend to pigeonhole our running into one time slot just like we are typically forced to pigeonhole everything else in order to manage our day.

We can reinvent our running to some extent by turning a spotlight on it by refitting it into a different segment of our day. When we do that, we tend to reinvent the priority of our run in the context of our average day so that it is no longer merely a mundane activity, one that is done almost robotically. If we set up the run in a different time frame, we are forced not only to accommodate it, but to consciously anticipate it.

Perhaps the most creative way to make the run suddenly noteworthy each day is to schedule it at a different time each weekday: early morning Monday, noon on Tuesday, late afternoon Wednesday, rest day Thursday, and early evening Friday.

The point is to raise the run above the expected, above the routine, in the process experimenting with the possibility that the time of day you have been doing your runs may not be the best time for you to be running, based on your circadian rhythms.

Experiment.

Change Your Courses

We've already mentioned this one, but it is more than worth repeating. There is nothing so deadly to your running as running the same few courses over and over and over. The older a runner you are, the more likely this applies to you. The most scenic course in the world run too many times has the blood drained from it.

For most of us who have busy lives, the most convenient way to run is out the front door at home or out the back door at work, using courses that are handy. If we're retired, our choice of doors seems diminished. Certainly, there is nothing wrong with that, especially when time is of the essence and you're lucky to get a run in at all! There is a tendency, though, to slip into the course of least resistance, again mindlessly running the same several courses.

When I worked at *Runner's World* in the late 1970s and early 1980s, the offices were on the wrong side of California Highway 101. Although we didn't have shower facilities at work, half the employees would head off on runs over the lunch hour. From the air, I'm sure it looked like mice deserting a sinking ship. Runners would stream out three or four different doors, and head off in wildly different directions. Unfortunately, the same runners would always head out onto the same courses.

After a few months of this, a group of us decided to have some fun with our noontime run by hooking up with a different group each day, running their courses instead of our own. It added tremendous variety to our runs, doubly so because once we got two groups together, there was more of

© Ken Lee

a tendency to go exploring even more courses, courses *none* of us had tried before.

The most memorable runs were with the handful of ultrarunners, who took pains to find the ugliest courses possible. The Methane Mountain run, for example, was through a deserted landfill where basketball-thick vent pipes had been pushed into the earth to allow the fermenting methane gases to escape. From the highest point—the peak of Methane

Mountain, a mere 50 feet above the surrounding landscape—we could see across San Francisco Bay all the way to Oakland. We had Methane Mountain all to ourselves. Of course, if a spark ever set off the escaping gases, the next issue of *Runner's World* would never have hit the stands, because half the staff would have been barbecued.

By combining portions of courses you already use, you can create new, fresh courses. Run courses backwards and the entire texture changes. Hook up with other runners and learn their courses. Or run alfresco—give yourself a certain amount of time and go exploring.

Reinvent your running courses, and you reinvent your running.

Change Your Specialty

Waldemar Cierpinski, a product of the East German Sports Federation, won the Olympic marathon in 1976 and 1980, only the second man in history to win Olympic marathon gold twice. The extremely efficient East German Sports Federation was in the habit of steering youngsters toward the sports for which they were best suited. Unfortunately for poor Waldemar, they pegged him as a steeplechase runner, and not an especially outstanding one at that. Fortunately for poor Waldemar, while on vacation in Czechoslovakia, he decided to enter a marathon, accidentally happening upon the event that would ultimately make him a household name in the world of sports. Obviously, had Cierpinski stayed on track with the life the Sports Federation had picked for him, he would have ended up unheralded and unknown.

It is daunting to realize how many recreational runners pigeonhole themselves into one or the other running and racing specialty—to the exclusion of all others. The incredible popularity of the 5K and 10K and the marathon stands in stark contrast to the unpopularity of cross-country and track running among recreational runners. To believe that everyone has in the glamour distances found his or her niche in running is such a stretch of the imagination that it isn't worth contemplating. Each year literally hundreds of thousands of mature runners compete at the 5K and 10K distances on the roads. And each year, a few of them are lured or stumble onto tracks where masters' and veterans' competition is going on—and they find they love it. The same is true of cross-country running and of ultramarathoning.

One of the best ways to reinvent your running is to reinvent your event and your terrain. Trying a new distance on different terrain is a sure way of pumping new blood into your running program. But, unfortunately, it often literally takes the intervention of a running friend to cajole the average older runner into trying a different form of running and racing.

It is no accident that a greater proportion of runners doing ultramarathons are older runners. They are runners who became tired of the mass races, who have learned how to pace themselves better and are therefore more suited to races that cover 50 or 100 miles, and who were looking for a new challenge.

And although most recreational runners tend to hate it, don't overlook the track as a viable alternative. There are extensive track programs around the world for 50+ runners. And some of the stars of the masters' and veterans' track world are people who never stepped onto a track until they were well past 40 years of age.

Don't overlook anything as a possible running venue. Try it all. Like poor Waldemar, you may well have been misdirected in your running and racing efforts. It's never too late to take up a new running career.

If You Race, Don't; if You Don't, Do

Now, in the wake of advising you to try different types of racing you haven't yet explored, some contrary advice. To reinvent your running, to revitalize it, you may want to consider giving up racing for a while, or at least cutting back on it.

Many runners find themselves on a racing treadmill and can't seem to get off. They go to a few races, then add a few more, then compulsively race every weekend. They become like the civic-minded retired fellow who used to live in our

© Ken Lee

condo complex: his calendar made him agitated if there was even one block on it that was empty; he compulsively scheduled meeting after meeting until every block on every month's page on the year's calendar was filled in — and then complained that he had no time to do anything he wanted to do.

Racing is a wonderful icing on the running cake, but it's something to be savored sparingly, not turned into a steady diet. Racing takes a great deal out of the body. And the older body needs more time and rest to come back from racing than the younger body does. The prevailing theory is that we should give ourselves one easy day of running or one rest day for each mile raced. For older runners, the figures should be doubled. Race a 10K this weekend, and you shouldn't race again for two weeks. Run a marathon, and you shouldn't race for two months.

We need to respect and revere our bodies, not abuse them. And although running is a positive force, like anything else, it can be perverted into something negative if we compulsively overdo it. If you race regularly, you can reinvent your running program by taking six months or a year to run strictly recreationally, leaving the racing alone.

On the other hand, you can radically reinvent your running by taking up racing if you are currently strictly a recreational runner. Indeed, racing is the icing on a person's running program. Racing can bring the running program to a head and add an entirely new dimension to the whole running experience. But again, it should be approached cautiously—don't overdo it. But do try it. It may end up being the highlight of your week.

Walk

Real runners don't walk. That's the attitude of the hard-core, die-hard runner. Anyone who walks when they're supposed to be running is a wimp. Even Oprah Winfrey ran every step of the Marine Corps Marathon when she made her marathon debut.

Fortunately, there is the occasional voice of sanity in the desert of mindless dedication. Most "real" runners who advocate the no-walking approach to running haven't got a very sound historical perspective of human locomotion. In the 19th century there was a breed of professional human locomotor known as the "pedestrian." Pedestrians regularly covered 100 miles in less than 24 hours, more than 500 miles in six days. Literally thousands of people paid to come and see them compete. In March of 1879, the third Astley Belt competition (a six-day, go-as-you-please race) was held at Madison Square

Garden. Ten thousand people paid to see four peds race around an indoor oval, while thousands more pounded on the doors to be allowed inside.

In the 1960s, American ultramarathoning pioneer Tom Osler, a math professor at a New Jersey college, worked walking into his running as he competed at 24-hour track races. More recently, 1972 Olympian and 50+ runner Jeff Galloway and former *Runner's World* editor and 50+ runner Joe Henderson give seminars to thousands of runners a year explaining how they can improve their running by working walking into their training and racing.

John Keston, of Oregon by way of the U.K., set a world age-group record by running/walking a 3:00:58 marathon at age 71. John uses brisk walking workouts several times a week to keep up his aerobic fitness while gentling his body through additional training mileage and in the process massaging soreness out of leg muscles.

If you don't currently use walking as part of your running program, you may want to reinvent your program—and in the process increase your longevity as a runner. On training runs and races, consider brisk walking for every tenth minute of your workout or race. The practice allows you to go farther than you're used to, and recovery time is cut way back.

Remember that it isn't as though using walking to run better is something new or revolutionary; it's just something that occasionally gets overlooked. And real runners do walk:

• In the 1975 Boston Marathon, Bill Rodgers walked through several aid stations so that he could drink fluids without spilling them; he also stopped in the middle of the road late in the race to tie his shoelace. He ran 2:09:55, at that time a new American marathon record.

• Tim Twietmeyer has four times won the grueling Western States 100, a 100-mile trail race that runs over the Sierra Nevada range in California. He concedes that he walks at least 15 percent of the course. That translates to 15 miles or more of the 100-mile race. And yet he wins.

Consider working walking into your running. It's an innovative training technique that's older than any of us.

Reversing

> *"Worrying about getting old*
> *is senseless. Worrying about*
> *something that is inevitable only*
> *serves to run us down faster.*
> *We deteriorate when we worry;*
> *that is why I do the opposite*
> *of worry: I take action."*

—Helen Klein

Change freaks out most people. Even the prospect or the rumor of change is enough to get some people agitated and sweaty. Yet other people thrive on change. Inevitably, however, age dampens the passion for change in even the most adventurous. In those who feared change all their lives, the very hint of change at a mature age can be psychologically devastating.

But if there is one constant in the world, it is change. It is tempting to make a bald statement like this: Change is good. And philosophically, it is. It has to be. Or else the world and the people in it would stagnate. Although it has its share of stick-in-the-muds, America's history has been driven in large part by people seeking and instigating change. If it hadn't, we'd all be even more consumed by the foibles of the English Royal Family than some of us are, because we'd still be a motley group of colonies.

Fortunately for those of us who are aging—and there are precious few beyond Jack LaLanne who aren't—a segment of Americans are throwing off the silly notion that as you age, you should prepare yourself to go gently into the night. More and more Americans are assaulting aging with physical activity, and not surprisingly, the psychological barriers against such physical pursuits are being ripped apart while the medical community sprints to catch up. More and more studies indicate that just because someone is aging doesn't mean he or she should curtail physical activities. To the contrary, aging people should become more active if they hope to continue performing even the simplest tasks. Jack LaLanne said it best: use it or lose it.

Cut the Chains

The philosophical and psychological chains of doing less as we age have been cut and discarded. Change is in the air. Hard-core resistance exercises performed by 80- and 90-year-olds have seen those same seniors throwing away their canes and walkers and recapturing control of their own lives.

Change can revive and reverse a faltering running program. In the previous chapter we discussed changing your specialty. This chapter is an expansion of that concept. A call for the Renaissance Runner, if you will.

Although the runners I admire most (Emil Zatopek and Abebe Bikila) are from a previous era, one of my heroes of the "modern" era is Rod Dixon. His range as a runner was marvelous. Not only did he break four minutes for the mile, but at the New York City Marathon in 1983, he broke 2:10! Talk about range. Rod Dixon never encountered an opportunity he didn't take. We can do the same, in the process reversing ourselves to save and revitalize our running.

Too many mature runners who have gravitated to ultramarathoning and discovered the joys of trail running have in the process completely disavowed the roads. Many who have entered running at a mature age have answered the siren song of the marathon and have been addicted to 26.2 miles to the exclusion of all other distances. Some who have spent most of their running lives on the track scorn the roads as impure

and imprecise. And often road racers who have led careful lives, but lives of accomplishment, look with horror at the mud, grime, and depravity of cross-country running and racing.

Yet in each specialty is a wonderful opposite or reversal waiting to be used to complement or invigorate one's running.

Think about it. The precise, antiseptic microcosm of the 5,000 meters on the track has an evil twin: the 5K cross-country race, especially if it is run a day or two after a torrential downpour, or better yet, *during* the torrential downpour! The overall downhill, fully paved, fully certified Las Vegas International Marathon has a multitude of evil clones: dozens of mountain marathons that are marginally measured and certifiably dangerous due to slippery rocks, grasping vines and roots, and segments much too narrow for safe passing. The one-mile track run has an evil, inbred cousin or two lurking about: one-mile track relays, 24-hour relays, 24-hour runs where ultrarunners who wouldn't go to a track on a bet to do repeat miles will run around the same track for 24 hours straight.

That's the beauty of running. For something so incredibly simple, it has virtually no limits. By its very simplicity, it invites creativity and renewal by being ready, willing, and able to reverse itself at a moment's notice. There is nothing that will keep a running program so alive as to constantly explore running's limits and limitlessness.

Explore Your Opposites

And the simplest way to immediately instigate that process is to reverse yourself. In so doing you may find, like Waldemar Cierpinski found when he chanced upon the marathon, that you've spent too many years away from the running event where your real talents lie. Just because all your friends are doing marathons, doesn't mean that you are a born marathoner. Your forte may be mountain running or the 10K or the mile. Unfortunately, most runners gravitate to one or two events and never explore the other possibilities; as though born to a specific religion, they are bonded to that one religion for life.

It would be quite easy to fill the rest of this chapter with a chart that would, on the left, list running events, and on the right, list their opposites, so that you could run your finger down the left side, find where you have been spending your time, then run your finger across the page to find what you might try to reverse and revive your running. But you can literally make your own customized list. The process can be fun. Let's throw out a half-dozen:

Currently Running	*Logical Opposite*
Marathon, paved roads	Cross-country
Mile, track	Mountain marathon
Marathon relay	Medley relay, track
Corporate Challenge	Hood-to-Coast Relay
400 meters, track	Adventure run (chapter 25)
Half marathon, roads	Half marathon, trails

The list is nearly endless because the sport has no boundaries.

Nearly two decades after the fact, I can vividly recall the year I ran every distance from the 400 meters to 50 miles, not all of it well, but certainly memorably if it sticks in my mind all these years later. The regular track workouts (in training for the Corporate Cup Relays) combined with the long, slow distances (50K through 50 miles) must have combined to some good end because it was the year I set PRs (personal records) in the mile, the 10K, and the marathon.

And that's the other often overlooked (psychological) aspect for the mature runner: as we age, we naturally become slower. Our PRs become a thing of the past, and we face the daunting prospect of never seeing another PR, unless we break them down into age-group records. By changing distances and surfaces in midstream, we open a whole new record book on which we can write new PRs.

If you've never run cross-country, you have no PR. The record book is waiting with a blank page to record not just the PR you establish the first time you run the event, but subsequent PRs as you learn the discipline and the tricks of the new venue. You can literally contemplate several years of racing your new event in which PRs are not only possible, but probable.

And the longer the distance of the new event, the more chances there are for continued PRs simply because there is more distance over which to learn new approaches and advanced training methods, and in which you can use your mature pacing techniques. Never run a 50-miler? An entire world awaits you: a world in which you can literally improve for years to come as you learn the proper training methods and the tricks of the trade. It's no accident that the longer the distance in running, the higher the average age of the participants. The wisdom of good pacing comes with maturity, and there is no way to run a creditable 50-miler without an intimate knowledge of pacing.

Change Comes; There's No Stopping It

Change is going to happen. It happens every day. There is no way to stop it. We have two options: to be "victims" of change, kicking and screaming and whining all the way, or to get a jump on and embrace the change in our lives by instigating some of it ourselves before it has a chance to instigate itself. That way we have some control over exactly what the change is and what outcome to expect.

Take the time to sit down and evaluate your running program. Is it still fresh, invigorating, a positive force in your life? If it isn't as fresh as you'd like, instead of waiting around for something miraculous to happen, take matters into your own hands, and reverse your running program in order to revive it. You'll literally be shocked at the positive effects such changes can have on your running program and, as a result, on your life in general.

For every 1,000 stick-in-the-muds, there is a rebel out there, a person who not only endures change, but relishes it. I hesitate to bring up the next subject in polite, general company, even if it is among fellow runners, because it is a relatively well-guarded secret and is certainly not for everyone. But it is certainly a step that, once taken, can never be reversed, and a step that will decidedly reshape your running—and your life.

A Four-Letter Word
Starting With *H*

I am tempted to add a disclaimer here for my own protection and yours, but instead will merely warn the gentle reader that only the truly lost should venture beyond this paragraph. All who value their sanity should turn back for their own well-being and for the peace of their family and friends.

The subject I am about to discuss would be, to some, distasteful—even tasteless. But those with weak constitutions and conservative self-images have already headed back to safer ground, so press in a bit closer and we'll mutter the maniacal words that have reversed and revived many a running career:

Hash House Harriers. Sssssshhhhh! Not so loud. Utter the words at your own peril. Hash House Harriers. Running's dirty (literally) secret.

Begun by a group of Brits in 1938 while stranded and bored in Kuala Lumpur, Malaysia back when Britain still had an empire, the Hash House Harriers are a loosely cobbled-together running club with 1,100 chapters (called "hashes") around the world, over 200 of which are in the U.S. The club's

self-description is "a drinking club with a running problem."
Think *Animal House* on endorphins.

Although originally all-male, the HHH enthusiastically accepts anyone, regardless of gender, age, race, political affiliations, whatever. The only prerequisite is that you leave your stuffed shirt at home and that you arrive primed for craziness. The intent of the club is probably best summarized by the Delaware Hash Hotline: 302-NEED-FUN.

One of the most fun things HHHers do (besides drinking copious amounts of beer and partying) is a "hash," which is a variation of the old "hounds and hare" concept: one runner goes off in advance with marker ribbons and plots a course that may cover as little as two miles or as many as five; after a given amount of lead time, the hounds take off after the hare, following the ribbons. The hare, naturally, attempts to make the course as difficult—and often as dirty—as possible, all in hopes of slowing down the hounds. The hare sometimes resorts to leaving deceptive markers. The rule of the game, literally, is that there are no rules. It is not unusual for the course to enter one door in a bar and exit the other; since there are no rules, there is no rule against using the bar as an aid station. Some famed, or infamous, hashes have been known to run through the smoking room of fancy downtown hotels after having crossed a muddy stream, and one hash used the main reading room of the Library of Congress as part of its course.

The hash usually finishes at a bar or at the home of a member, where copious amounts of beer are consumed, the beer used to wash down tacos or some other post-hash delicacy. Of course, since there are no rules in the HHH, members aren't required to drink beer; they can drink whatever they like, even tea, and some do. Whatever your drink, when it's your turn for punishment, and the command "Down-down!" is barked, you're required to either quaff the entire contents of your mug or pour what you couldn't get down over your head. Makes a good case for abstaining from Gatorade.

The Hash House Harriers are unabashedly a channel for reversing the direction of your mortal body and immortal soul in one fell swoop. It's a perfect excuse to embark, in a BIG way, on your second childhood, by way of running.

If you have access to the World Wide Web (or if you have a grandchild who does), it's a convenient resource of HHH information. Call up the website "Hash The World!", which lists HHH events around the world through the year 2002. Here's the address: Hash The World!, 2225 Armacost Dr., Henderson, NV 89014, phone 702-263-3388, fax 702-263-4487, or e-mail at hash-1@usc.edu. Get ready for fun.

chapter

24

Imagining

*"The mind is the limit. As long
as the mind can envision the fact
that you can do something,
you can do it—as long
as you really believe 100 percent."*

—Arnold Schwarzenegger

Many adult runners short-sheet their potential accomplishments in running because they have never made the mental transition to think of themselves as athletes. This is understandable. Natural-born and coddled athletes are recognized early and are never granted the latitude to think of themselves as anything else but a natural athlete, so they grow up and nourish that impression of themselves, and it is further nourished on a daily basis by our sports-addled society.

Most of us, however, especially those of us who gravitated to running well beyond our formative years, have not been grounded in athlete-think. We tend to think of ourselves more as plodders or practitioners, not as running animals capable of incredible feats.

The reason is three-pronged:

1. We generally came to the sport later in life and therefore were not identified with our running accomplishments from an early age and did not therefore identify ourselves with sport.

2. Running, unlike sports demanding some degree of hand-eye coordination, is not taken seriously as a sport by most of our society, if for no other reason than virtually anyone can run, at least passingly.

3. The problem is further complicated by this fact: the people likely to become involved in running later in life are generally goal-oriented and accomplished individuals who are used to pushing themselves toward perfection by being highly self-critical. What this translates to is that coming to running later in life, you've missed the critical nurturing formative years, and are now required by your upbringing to compare yourself and your running to those who've been doing it most of their lives, are generally much younger than you, have confidence coming out of every pore, and are therefore much better at running and racing.

It's no wonder we don't think of ourselves as athletes and therefore do not think as athletes do. We've never been taught how.

Know How to Be Critical

What we do know how to do, however, is to be very hypercritical of our performances on all levels of life, because we've learned over the years that by carefully and clinically examining our performance in other areas of our lives, especially in the area of our professional accomplishments, we are able to overcome shortcomings by shining a spotlight on them and working diligently on them in order to improve. We tend to examine the failures, correct the mistakes, and move gradually toward the positive.

Unfortunately, with running, the mature runner who follows this scenario is creating a situation for failure. What tends to be stressed is the negative, the reasons why you'll fail, and they are all reasons with a certain logical validity attached to them: I haven't had enough time to get in the critical workouts, I'm 30 years older than the top guns, I've got a half-dozen other priorities hanging over my head that need attention paid to them.

Considering all the baggage the older runner brings to running, it is a wonder he or she runs halfway decently at all, ever. Because, coming from the negative, critical side, we are unsparingly honest if not always realistic, and we fulfill our negative estimations of our lack of prowess while usually overlooking our strengths.

It isn't easy to make the transition to listing all the positive aspects of your recent running that will contribute to your doing a good job at Sunday's race: last weekend's long run went well, the Thursday track session with the club went well, the weatherman says Sunday is going to be my kind of weather, the race is being run on one of my favorite courses, I'm 30 years older than the open competitors so I'm not competing against them at all but rather against my contemporaries (although I may beat some of the open runners in the process), and when I get home I can run my time through the age-adjusted tables and see where I would have placed had I been 30 years younger.

Our upcoming performances should be based on the quality of our past performances and recent workouts, not on a litany of negatives that need attention but that are guaranteed to defeat us.

Jogger Versus Runner

This gulf is, in a sense, the difference between "jogger" and "runner." Over the years, there have been many attempts at defining the difference between the jogger and the runner, much of it unrealistically based upon the number of minutes it took the subject to cover one mile. The difference, however, is a matter of attitude toward the sport. The person who laboriously plods through three miles three times a week as a prescription for health is a jogger. Even the person who plods through a full marathon may be a jogger if there is no inner-based urge for improvement.

This phenomenon reaches its silly pinnacle at races where a 70-year-old who places seventh in an age-group of eight berates the race director because there is no seventh-place trophy in the 70-and-above age group. This person attempts to demand a trophy for merely existing. The first-place winner in this runner's age group may have finished the course in half the time, and with some work, our seventh-place finisher might improve his performance enough to place in the awards, but the transition from jogger to runner to racer often never occurs because it requires some additional work—but more importantly, it requires a reassessment of one's self. The difference between this person's first and seventh may be due in some part to genes, but on a larger plane, the difference is defined by attitude, by approach, by focus, by hard work, and by imagining himself to be a good runner, and then working toward it.

Surprisingly, it can sometimes be less work and more fun to approach one's running at a higher level than at a lower, seemingly easier level. It is certainly more fulfilling and, if the older runner carefully monitors workouts and includes sufficient rest and some walking for active recovery, it may be possible to reduce injuries simply because the runner is running more effectively and efficiently. Running slowly is not usually running efficiently.

How does one imagine oneself to be a better runner and then make it happen? Certainly not by totally ignoring shortcomings. The world champion runner wins by assessing his or her shortcomings and then training around them and overwhelming the shortcomings by downplaying them and then by spending most of his or her energy building upon the positives.

The process is a matter of practical application of good training meeting the imagining of yourself as the best runner you can be. Imagining yourself as the best runner you can be is not some hocus-pocus or some New Age nonsense. If the imagining is based upon very real, very measurable workouts, if the imagining is based upon very real performance numbers on certain courses as you approach an important competition, if the imagining is based upon gradual improvements over the years, the imagining becomes the glue that holds the tangibles together on race day.

This process is often referred to as "visualization." I prefer to use the word "imagining" because it infers that you are creating in your mind that which has not been but that is practical based upon your workouts and potential. Imagining, therefore, more easily covers the mature runner who has not always seen him- or herself as an athlete, while "visualization" infers making a mental picture of what you already know from experience to be possible.

Imagining = Rehearsal

The imagining is essentially a rehearsal, very much like a Broadway play the month leading up to opening night. You can try this on regular workouts. It doesn't have to be applied only to an extremely important race.

If you have a five-mile course you use once a week, begin to keep track of your performances on that course over a period of a few months. If you are building to a specific competition, you can begin to use the five-mile course as an indicator of how fit and how fast you are. By imagining exactly how you want that five-mile workout to go a day in advance, then reviewing (rehearsing) it several times in your mind, as long as your imagining is realistic based upon your current level of fitness, you can learn, in a noncompetitive environment, to realize reality out of imagining—as long as that imagining is based upon realistic performances to that point.

The first step, however, is to make the great leap away from the self-critical approach. Play down your negatives and put some faith in your positives. Consider that your positives are almost always very measurable (I did 31:45 for that tough five-mile course on Thursday) while your negatives are often more vaporous (I don't feel I've got the leg speed to do 31:45 on that five-mile course, although I did it in 31:58 last week after staying out too late the night before).

Try it. You've got nothing to lose. It is especially easy to apply imagining to courses you run on a regular basis because you are so intimately acquainted with the course and with your past performances on the course and you have a realistic idea of your potential performance.

Try the imagining first with your favorite course. By doing this, you'll feel you *already* have an advantage going into it, because you already like the course. You needn't become obsessed with thinking constantly about tomorrow's run on that course. Just take two minutes several times a day and "run" yourself through it, hitting the highlights. You don't need to spend 45 minutes running a tough 10K course step by step in your imagination. Once this technique is practiced enough, it tends to reach the point where you will eagerly anticipate the run when its time comes.

As you can imagine, the technique works wonderfully for races, as long as you have a working knowledge of the course, so that you can imagine key approaches to various course characteristics: how will your regular hill repeats translate to the hills at 18 miles in the marathon course? Can you translate the 2-mile straight on your favorite 10-mile course to the 2-mile straight at 21 miles in the marathon?

The Real-World Computer Game

Think of your imagining as the ultimate computer action game: you've played the same game a dozen times, you know all the ins and outs, all the tricks the course is likely to throw at you and your logical responses, but unlike a computer game, where the game stays in the computer, you now have the opportunity to take the game outside and apply it to the very real asphalt roads. It is simply a process of turning virtual reality into real-world reality.

The secret is to be willing to make the shift in how you view yourself as a runner, stress the positives, and then realistically imagine your training logically applied to a real-life training or racing situation.

Remember that this technique works not because it is a trick, but because it is an outcome built on realistic input from your weekly training. In a sense, it is merely translating current reality into the next logical reality. It works. It's how world-class runners win races and set world records. And it is how you can bump your running and racing program up to the next very satisfying plateau.

Pioneering

*"He conquers
who endures."*

—Persius

Even though the fact that 60,000 runners take part in the Bay-to-Breakers in San Francisco and the Bloomsday Race in Spokane, nearly 30,000 run the Honolulu Marathon, and more than that many run the New York City Marathon makes it seem that much of running today is faceless, no one race is right for every runner. For some people who run simply to run, no race at all is right for them.

When a runner has run for literally decades and has perhaps done it all, or as nearly "all" as any runner can, a definite attitude toward what works and what doesn't for that particular runner will have developed in his or her mind. This attitude of "Is that all there is?" is not uncommon among older runners who've been there, done that, and who are looking for new challenges and new horizons. Which is why so many older runners are stepping up to ultrarunning, where the run is literally to the next horizon, and sometimes beyond.

A well-developed objective assessment of what works and what doesn't work for a runner from years and decades of running is an invitation to take the ultimate stride: toward developing a customized adventure run as a long-term goal and affirmation of running. For the 50+ runner who has literally done it all in running, the customized ultramarathon or adventure run is the ultimate giant stride.

Two Kinds of Runners, Lots of Possibilities

Unfortunately, there are two kinds of runners who contemplate the ultimate run: independent adventurers and those who aren't. Fortunately, those who "aren't," who feel they need an established structure inside which they can function, aren't left out in the cold these days, because there are a number of worthwhile adventure run experiences organized by others into which the not-so-independent runner can plug. We'll come back to that alternative later.

But let's focus first on the pure, true adventure run as a worthy long-term, ultimate goal for the 50+ runner who, well, has already tried just about everything there is to do in running.

For an adventure run to be worth doing, it must meet certain criteria:

- It is doable, but damned challenging. The more challenging the run can be made—within reasonable limits—the better. What's the sense of doing something that's easy?

- It allows the runner, under his or her own power, to travel somewhere unique—or somewhere the runner has always wanted to go.

- A great deal of organizational skill is involved in putting the run together, organizing a support crew, and pulling the run off under whatever conditions present themselves.

- The runner will need a bunch of help from his or her friends, and in the process each participant will learn something important about him- or herself and about the others involved in the adventure.

- In order to build to it properly, the runner will need at least a year of planning and special training, and perhaps more.

If the way a true adventure run is posed sounds more like the Normandy Invasion than like a running experience, it's because that's just what it is: an invasion into "fringe" territory.

The Adventure Run

So just what are we talking about when we use the term "adventure run"? It's easier to give examples than attempt to describe them, since the very concept of a true adventure run makes the entire concept open-ended. Here are a few examples:

- Run the length of your home state. Of course, that makes such a challenge relatively easy on East Coast runners as opposed to Mountain Time Zone runners.
- Run the entire length of the Appalachian Trail, or at least a significant part of it.
- Run the route of the Pony Express.
- Run a 200-mile segment of the Lewis and Clark Expedition.
- Run the length of the Mississippi River.
- Run the route of the overland gold rush of 1896 from Edmonton, Alberta, Canada, to Dawson City in the Yukon Territory.
- Run the Alcan Highway.
- Run the route of the California missions from San Diego to Sonoma, attempting to reach the next of the 22 missions at the end of each day.
- Run the John Muir Trail through the High Sierra.
- Run around the border of Wyoming . . . or South Dakota . . . or Idaho . . . or whatever.
- Near San Francisco Bay, circle the entire Bay Area by running to the peak of all four major mountains in the area: Mt. Diablo, Mt. St. Helena, Mt. Tamalpias, Mt. Hamilton.
- Run through the capitals of each of the 13 original American colonies.

You get the idea.

The Plan, the Execution

The beauty of such a major enterprise is that it's entirely *your* major enterprise. If it's an adventure run that's never to your knowledge been done before, so much the better. You become the first, Numero Uno.

The challenges that face you now are these:

1. Scope out and study the proposed run. Determine what permits and permissions (if any) will be needed, and map

out the route, noting the specific challenges the course offers.

2. Persuade a group of your friends to buy into your revolutionary vision to serve as crew. Pick the one who is the best organized and the best leader to serve as crew chief.

3. Formulate a logical training program built specifically around the unique challenges the proposed course provides.

4. Give yourself sufficient time to train for the run. Be realistic. For some such runs, a year's worth of training and planning may not be enough.

5. With your crew chief's help, begin amassing the supplies, maps, clothing, vehicles, motel reservations, and so on needed for your assault on your adventure run.

6. Be flexible. At some point during the actual adventure run, things will likely come a bit undone. Be prepared to move quickly to accommodate changes in plans.

7. Well before you leave on your adventure run, finalize plans for a post-run celebration in which you can attempt, in some small way, to pay back the time and effort your support crew puts into this effort.

8. Be honest in training. If a shot at a successful crossing of your course demands a series of grueling workouts two months before, do the grueling runs. Don't go to the course with half your workouts undone. It's unfair to your crew—and to the course you've picked out—to go to it unprepared. To do so jeopardizes you, your crew, and the entire enterprise. And your crew will never talk to you again for the rest of your life if you string them along and then put in a half effort.

9. Be nice to your crew. They're being nice to you by even showing up to help you.

A well-run adventure run can open doorways to the interior of a runner he or she never knew existed. It can serve as an arena in which people who've known each other for years and people who have been acquainted for only months develop a bond that is available today only in serious, drawn-out crisis situations. And it definitely puts your running on a whole 'nother plane in your life, sometimes to the point that your everyday running in the wake of the adventure run is done on another level, sometimes because the adventure run was so severe at times that an everyday run with none of the challenges of the adventure run becomes something precious.

It would be easy to write a 50,000-word guide to preparing for an adventure run. The guide would contain checklists, cautions, training tips (take progressively larger running shoes along because your feet tend to swell the longer you're on them), advice for crews, vehicle preparation advice, and so on. But to provide such a guide would to some degree undermine the challenge of researching and preparing for the adventure from the ground up. The preparation, the anticipation, is one of the aspects of the individual-originated adventure run that makes it such a special experience.

The fact that you took the time and the effort to plan out every aspect of the adventure run gives you that much more satisfaction for a job well done when the run is finished.

For the Less Adventurous

Some runners are not inclined to put together an entire adventure run from the ground up. If you are one of those folks, signing up for a group adventure run in a foreign country you've always wanted to visit might be a viable alternative. The satisfaction of having put everything together yourself will not be there, but then you won't have to trouble yourself by doing a lot of planning and dealing with unexpected headaches along the way, because the organizer will have done all that work for you. And, since there will be other adventurous people on the trip with you, you will have the opportunity to meet and meld with other like-minded runners.

Besides foreign adventures, of which there are a fair number offered these days (check the classified ad pages of magazines such as *Outside* and *Runner's World*), there are also a number of adventure races organized by various groups. One of the most famous of these is the Hi-Tec Badwater 135 race from Badwater in the depths of Death Valley to Whitney Portal on the side of Mt. Whitney. Begun in 1988, the race is run in July, runners must qualify to enter the race, it is very arduous (especially since the start was moved to the morning in 1996), and you've still got to organize your own support crew, but it is an experience not soon forgotten.

Adventure races like this will test your soul, but older runners tend to do quite well in them because when it comes to an adventure run, pacing is everything, and mature runners usually became mature runners and not nonrunners by using their heads when it comes to pacing.

Even for an organized adventure run, however, it is imperative that you train properly, read all of the available literature, and take the run ultra-seriously because your life—and the lives of others—may depend on it. It is not a stretch, however, to say that participating in an adventure run can be one of the most exhilarating experiences a runner can have. For some runners, it provides the cherry on top of the icing on top of the cake (see the sidebar on Helen Klein on page 12).

In the wake of a challenging adventure run, your regular running will never be the same—and neither will you. The adventure run can be the experience the 50+ runner needs to literally turbocharge running through the second half-century of life. Explore the limits of your limits. If there are any.

Index

About the Author

Richard Benyo is the editor of *Marathon & Beyond* and race
director of the Sutter Home Napa Valley Marathon. He's also
a serious long-distance runner who over the past 20 years has
competed in practically every type of running event imaginable—from 400-meter runs to ultramarathons. This veteran of
more than 35 marathons became the first person, along with
Tom Crawford, to run from Death Valley to the peak of Mount
Whitney and back in midsummer—a distance of 300 miles.
Rich was the executive editor of *Runner's World* during the
height of the running boom, from 1977 to 1984, and the fitness
and running columnist for the *San Francisco Chronicle* from
1985 to 1990. He is the author of *Masters of the Marathon, The
Exercise Fix*, and *Making the Marathon Your Event*. A member
of the Road Runners Club of America, Rich currently lives in
Forestville, CA, with his wife Rhonda Provost.

ADDITIONAL BOOKS FOR RUNNERS FROM HUMAN KINETICS

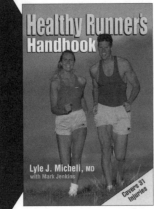

1996 • Paper • 264 pp
Item PMIC0524 • ISBN0-0-88011-524-6
$16.95 ($24.95 Canadian)

Sports physician Lyle J. Micheli helps you put an end to nagging overuse injuries and continue running safely and successfully. *Healthy Runner's Handbook* shows you how to diagnose, care for, and rehabilitate 31 common overuse injuries and provides useful advice on how to prevent such injuries.

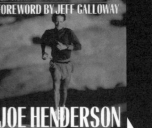

1996 • Paper • 264 pp
Item PHEN0866 • ISBN 0-87322-866-9
$14.95 ($19.95 Canadian)

Joe Henderson draws on his years of running and writing experience to share what he and others have learned about running over the past quarter century. *Better Runs* is filled with anecdotes and insights on training, racing, and more!

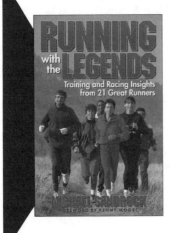

1996 • Paper • 592 pp
Item PSAN0493 • ISBN 0-87322-493-0
$19.95 ($29.95 Canadian)

Running with the Legends is a complete look at how running and runners have changed. Details the development, training techniques, coaching, competitions, motives, and perspectives of 21 all-time great runners.

HUMAN KINETICS
The Information Leader in Physical Activity
http://www.humankinetics.com/
2335

For more information or to place your order, U.S. customers call toll-free 1-800-747-4457. Customers outside the U.S. use the appropriate telephone number/address shown in the front of this book.